STIR FRY COOKING

Title

STIR FRY COOKING

BRIDGET JONES

THE
APPLE
PRESS

A QUINTET BOOK

Published by The Apple Press
6 Blundell Street
London N7 9BH

ISBN 1-85076-475-1

This book was designed and produced by
Quintet Publishing Limited
6 Blundell Street
London N7 9BH

Creative Director: Richard Dewing
Designers: Stuart Walden, Ian Hunt
Project Editor: William Hemsley
Illustrator: Syrah Arnold
Photographer: Trevor Wood

Typeset in Great Britain by
Central Southern Typesetters, Eastbourne
Manufactured in Singapore by Eray Scan Pte Ltd
Printed in Singapore by Star Standard Industries Pte Ltd

CONTENTS

FOREWORD

Stir frying is often classified, quite correctly, as a cooking method for oriental dishes or for 'healthy' meals since it is authentic to the first category and thoroughly appropriate to the second. However, in the pages that follow, I would like to demonstrate that the technique of stir frying can be as exotic or homely, as healthy or rich, and as simple or as complicated as you wish to make it.

The oriental origins have produced a distinct style of food preparation and mixing which has dominated stir fry cooking but, given that a few basic rules are followed, a range of multi-national dishes may be created. For beginners, there are notes on the choice of cooking equipment, from the ideal options through to improvising, and a few comments which may be helpful if you are thinking of buying a new stir fry pan. The rest of the introduction sets out simple guidelines for the choice of ingredients, the techniques for cutting and flavouring them,

and the importance of cooking different foods in the right order to achieve perfect results.

Hopefully, once you have read the opening pages you will appreciate the principles of this quick cooking method, so that you may look upon the recipes as a basis for extending your existing culinary repertoire and experimenting with new ideas or interesting seasonings.

Take advantage of the cornucopia of ingredients now available from all corners of the world – the exotic vegetables and fruit; fragrant spices and preserves; contrasting grains and cereals; and quick-to-cook seafood, poultry or meat. Look upon your stir fry pan as an essential item for practical or the latest cooking – whether to boost the healthy side of a balanced everyday diet or to conjure up fashionable meals in minutes – and it will soon become one of the best-used items in the kitchen. Here's to quick cooking and good eating – bon appetite!

INTRODUCTION

Utensils – Essential Equipment for Preparation and Cooking

The key piece of equipment is, of course, the cooking pan and the most important feature is size: a good stir fry pan must hold a large volume of ingredients, at the same time allowing sufficient room for stirring and turning them during cooking. The recipes do not give specific information on the type of pan because it is unnecessary; if you are new to stir frying, it would be a good idea to read the following notes before attempting the recipes.

Woks

A wok is the most suitable pan for the majority of stir frying but there is a choice of types, from traditional cook pans to electric appliances.

CARBON STEEL WOK The traditional wok is made from thin, uncoated carbon steel. It is deeply curved with a stout wooden handle, which is designed for lifting, tilting and shaking the pan using one hand, leaving the other hand free for using a scoop to stir the ingredients. The domed pan fits over a flaming brazier in Chinese restaurants, but at home a rack may be used to stabilize a wok on an electric hob, or if necessary, over a gas burner. However, depending on the pan stands on a gas hob, the rack may be redundant.

This traditional type of wok conducts heat well, provides a large surface area for cooking and it is highly responsive to changes in heat. However, a carbon steel wok must be used regularly and kept oiled to prevent rusting between use. A new pan should be washed in hot soapy water to remove any protective coating, then tempered or seasoned. This involves heating a small amount of oil in the wok, rubbing it over all the surface of the pan, until smoking hot but not burning. The pan should be wiped out with absorbent kitchen paper. The outside and any exposed metal around the edge of the handle must be oiled. Wipe with clean absorbent kitchen paper before storage or use. After each use, the pan must be wiped out and oiled before storage.

Two designs of wok, one with the traditional long wooden handle and the other with two carrying handles. The brush may be used to oil woks, and the strainers are useful accessories for some recipes.

Depending on the food cooked, there are two ways of cleaning the pan. Ideally, wipe out the pan with absorbent kitchen paper, then sprinkle in some salt and pour in a little oil. Heat this and remove the pan from the heat. Use a pad of absorbent kitchen paper to clean the wok – the salt acts as a scouring agent and removes food residues. Wipe out all the oil and salt, then heat the wok again with a little fresh oil before wiping it clean. If the food has left a cooked-on coating of sauce, the pan must be washed, dried and tempered. This method of scouring with oil and salt is best for the majority of oil-based stir frying.

I find the most practical way of storing a carbon steel wok is to keep it well greased in a large polythene bag with an elastic band around the handle. I reserve my carbon steel wok for oriental and vegetable stir fries, and for dishes with small amounts of meat and grains. The carbon steel pan is not suitable for stir frying fruit.

STAINLESS STEEL AND NON-STICK WOKS These are far easier to look after than a carbon steel pan. They may be washed in hot soapy water, dried and stored according to the manufacturer's instructions.

The quality of the pans varies enormously, in general they are all slightly less responsive to changes in heat than carbon steel. Unlike carbon steel woks, the cheapest of which (purchased in an oriental supermarket) is often the best, price is often a good indication of quality within this group.

Consider the shape of the pan – many are smaller than expected of an authentic wok and they may have very flat bases, putting them on a par with a frying pan rather than a wok. A pan with a small, quite flat base may not be the best buy and a large conventional frying pan with deep sides may provide more surface area for cooking. Before buying, check the using instructions that go with the pan because some non-stick finishes are not suitable for cooking over high heat, therefore they are not ideal for the majority of stir frying. Inexpensive non-stick finishes can deteriorate rapidly when used over high heat and when the food is stirred constantly (even using the correct non-stick coated utensils).

ELECTRIC WOKS I have little experience of these but was surprised with the quality of the results when I tested one model. I found the pan to be more responsive than I had expected and suitable for cooking large quantities. This may not be the purists option but a work-top appliance is useful in many kitchens. Remember to follow carefully the manufacturer's instructions for use and cleaning.

Frying pans and skillets

A wok is not essential for stir frying; a frying pan or skillet used for this purpose should be large, with deep sides. Ideally, opt for a pan with slightly sloping sides and a curved edge around the base – this allows the food to be turned easily. The term skillet is a slightly confusing one – it is sometimes the American term for the British frying pan or it may refer to a pan which is about 5 cm/2 in deep (or slightly larger), suitable for frying, with a lid. A large skillet is ideal for stir frying as the depth of the sides prevents food from spilling during stirring and cooking.

A sauté pan is usually large with deep sides and, since sautéing is similar to stir frying in that the food is cooked over high heat and stirred during cooking (although less vigorously), this type of pan is suitable for stir frying.

Heavy, non-stick coated cast iron pans may be used for stir frying, but usually they have to be heated slowly and kept over a medium rather than high heat. The manufacturer may state that the pan should not be heated empty, therefore a coating of oil or fat should be added. The pan may be used for stir frying once hot, but the heat is not as fierce and the pan is not as responsive, taking a long time to cool or react to changes in temperature. These pans are suitable for stir frying fruit or other ingredients that are not necessarily cooked over fierce heat.

FEATURES TO LOOK FOR IN A PAN

▌ Materials and finishes that withstand high heat.

▌ A large cooking surface and/or room for pushing cooked ingredients to one side (for example the sides of a wok).

▌ A pan with deep sides to prevent food spillages during stirring.

▌ A long, sturdy handle which is a poor conductor of heat so that it stays cool during cooking.

▌ A pan with a lid can be useful if you intend using stir frying as one part of a longer cooking process – avoid a carbon steel lid for a wok as it rusts easily; look for a domed steel lid.

MAKING DO – WHAT TO AVOID

Even though a wok may be the ideal, improvising is part of the fun and skill of cooking. If you literally own just one saucepan, given that it is designed for putting over high heat and it has a surface area large enough for the quantities of food, then go ahead and stir fry in it!

● Preparation and cooking utensils

The preparation of food is equally as important as the cooking technique, involving a good deal of cutting up.

CHOPPING BOARDS Have a very large chopping board that can be scrubbed in hot soapy water. For the sake of food safety and hygiene, remember that wood is absorbent and easily damaged, allowing food particles to be trapped and bacteria to grow. If you do have a wooden board, scrub it in very hot water, using a mild solution of bleach or an abrasive cleaner. Rinse and thoroughly dry it AFTER EVERY USE.

Plastic-based boards are non-absorbent, therefore less likely to be a food safety risk. However, these too must be scrubbed after each use to clean them.

An important point to remember is that the board must be sufficiently spacious to cut a large volume of ingredients. There is nothing more frustrating than trying to cut even-sized slivers when there is barely room to fit the point of a knife between ingredients on the surface of the board!

KNIVES A good knife is essential – select a medium or large cook's knife with a strong blade which sharpens to an acute cutting edge. Never buy a knife by looks and technical information alone – pick it up and feel it, hold it as though to cut and try to get a feeling for how it manoeuvres. Assess several different types of knives before buying, looking for one which feels well balanced and comfortable. Wooden handles may look attractive but they require care and attention if they are to last, and they are definitely not dishwasher proof – in fact they should never be left in water, except for a brief (but thorough) wash. Wood also needs oiling occasionally. If this is unlikely to suit your kitchen habits, a good-quality dishwasher proof knife may be the better option. Whichever you decide upon, look for a knife with a handle riveted to the blade.

To go with your knife, you need a good quality steel to sharpen it – look for one with a guard to protect your hand should the knife slip up to the handle. Some oriental supermarkets and hardware shops sell sharpening stones – look for one that has both coarse and fine sides.

There are different ways of using a steel: slide the knife blade along the surface, working away from you.

Start with the wide end of the blade above and at the top of the steel, then slide it down until the point of the knife is at the tip of the steel. Repeat with the knife underneath the steel to work on the upper edge of the knife's blade.

Alternatively, have the knife point at the top of the steel, then work down the steel until the top of the blade is at its tip. Repeat with the knife underneath the steel.

If you are very inexperienced with handling knives, or prone to accidents, then hold the steel vertical, with its point on a firm board or surface. Work the knife down its length – this avoids any danger of the knife slipping towards your wrist.

Whichever method you use, repeat the process several times until the knife blade is sharp, then wash and dry it before use. Sharpen knives frequently, in theory before each use and during use when cutting quantities of ingredients.

STIRRING UTENSILS A large scoop or flat metal spatula, both with strong handles, are the perfect partners for a carbon steel wok. If you are using a non-stick pan, you will need a suitable plastic or non-stick coated spatula or slice. A slotted spoon (or draining spoon) may be used instead.

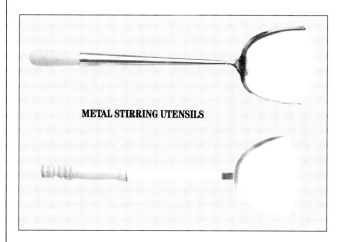

METAL STIRRING UTENSILS

ESSENTIAL ACCESSORIES Ingredients have to be prepared before you begin to stir fry them, so a selection of bowls or basins is useful for holding the ingredients. Cereal bowls or plastic containers may be used – the size and number depend on the dish being prepared.

Food at its Best – Selecting Ingredients

Quick cooking brings out the flavour of food to the full, but the right choice of ingredients is vital.

Fish and seafood

The majority of fish and seafood cooks quickly, so from the timing angle they are suitable for stir frying. However, thin fish fillets that break up easily during cooking are not suitable. Thicker portions of firm white fish, prawns, scallops, mussels, oysters and squid are all examples of seafood for stir frying.

Look for fresh fish which is moist, bright and firm. Avoid any that smells strong or looks dull and old. Buy from a reputable source and remember that the fishmonger will do a lot of the preparation for you.

Poultry

All types of poultry are suitable for stir frying because they cook quickly to give tender results. Prime cuts of breast fillet are best.

Meat

Tender cuts of meat recommended for grilling or frying are suitable for stir frying. Tougher pieces that require lengthy stewing or braising should be avoided. All pork is tender, but some cuts require more trimming to remove fat and gristle or sinews than others. Similarly, most cuts of lamb are suitable for stir frying, the prime choice being loin, fillet or leg meat.

Trim the excess fat and all gristle before cutting meat into thin pieces across the grain. Meat may be half frozen for easy slicing into paper-thin pieces.

Vegetables

The majority of vegetables may be stir fried for different lengths of time according to how quickly they cook. For example, root vegetables, such as potatoes, require longer cooking than beansprouts or Chinese leaves. The way in which the vegetables are cut also contributes to the cooking time.

Select very fresh vegetables in prime condition because second-rate ingredients are unsuitable for stir frying. Look for firm, unbruised vegetables with crisp leaves and a good colour. Avoid bruised or damaged specimens, root vegetables that are soft or wrinkled, and cabbages or other greens that are faded, yellowing or limp. Peppers, tomatoes and aubergines should be firm and bright.

Cereals, pulses and grains

Cooked cereals, beans and grains may be stir fried to make satisfying meals. It is important to avoid overcooking them before stir frying as they may break up or become very soft.

If these ingredients are cooked and cooled before stir frying, always ensure they are thoroughly reheated before serving to destroy any bacteria, which may have multiplied on cooling and during re-warming.

Fruit

Firm fruits respond well to stir frying and the softer types may be added during the final stages of cooking. Select perfect fresh fruit and prepare it just before cooking unless it is left to macerate as part of the recipe.

Dried and canned fruit are also suitable for stir frying – the types of dried fruit which are ready to eat are particularly useful.

Oils and fats

The choice of fat is important, not only for flavour but also for the results in cooking. Fats melt at different temperatures, for example, oil, lard, butter and margarine are all liquid at different temperatures.

When fats are heated chemical changes take place at varying temperatures, causing the fat to change in appearance and, eventually, flavour. If you have never noticed the way in which oils react to heating, then heat a few samples and watch. Butter tends to brown and burn at a lower temperature than some oils even though its melting temperature is higher.

Clarified butter is more suitable for frying as it does not break down as easily. It is prepared by melting the butter, then simmering it gently until a sediment forms and sizzling ceases. At this stage the solids are precipitated and the water content has evaporated (the sizzling continues until the water is driven off). The butter should be strained through muslin, then cooled before storage.

Margarines do not reach as high a cooking temperature and are not ideal for stir frying. Low fat spreads are not suitable for frying.

Olive oil smokes at a comparatively low temperature. It is useful for stir frying many ingredients or in dishes to which it contributes flavour.

Groundnut oil may be heated to a higher temperature before it begins to smoke. Therefore, it is ideal for cooking ingredients that benefit from rapid cooking and having a crisp outer surface.

Sunflower, corn and vegetable oils are all suitable, and they all reach temperatures high enough to make food brown and crisp. More importantly, they do not smoke and 'burn' too easily, and are therefore useful for prolonged frying at a high temperature.

Sesame oil and nut oils (walnut and hazelnut) are used for their flavour, but they overheat easily. Since they have distinct flavours, they are best used in small quantities as flavourings rather than the main cooking mediums. For example, a little of any one of these oils may be added to the mixture for meatballs or used in marinades, or a little sesame oil may be combined with sunflower or groundnut oil for cooking.

All-important Techniques

Stir frying is an easy, relaxed cooking method, which should not be dominated by pedantic do's and don'ts; however, the secret of success lies in efficient advance preparation of all ingredients. A few attempts at this cooking method is enough to make each cook their own expert.

Washing, draining and drying
Make sure all vegetables are clean before cutting and cooking. Some types are easier to wash after cutting, for example leeks. Drain most vegetables in a colander, small pieces in a sieve, and mop them on absorbent kitchen paper before cooking to prevent spitting.

Preparation and cutting
Stir frying is speedy, so all ingredients should be cut to cook quickly and evenly. The size of the pieces depends on the texture and cooking requirements of the food as much as on the expected result and appearance of the dish. Here is a list of some of the techniques used in the recipes.

SLICES Thick or thin, depending on how much cooking is required and the finished texture. Make sure slices are even.

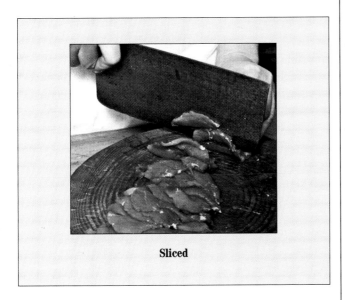
Sliced

DIAGONAL SLICES Cut into slices at an angle. For example, spring onions and celery sticks should have the end cut off at an angle, then all the slices should be cut at an angle to give evenly thick, slanting slices.

FINGERS OR STICKS Cut fairly thick slices, then cut these into fingers or sticks. Cucumber and courgettes should be cut into lengths, then quartered lengthways.

THIN STICKS Finer than fingers but not as delicate as matchstick strips, these are about 5 mm/¼ in thick.

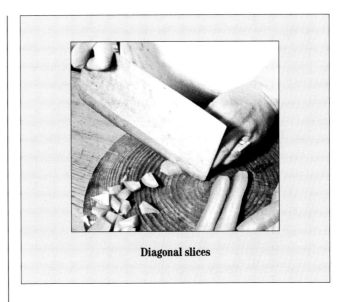
Diagonal slices

MATCHSTICK STRIPS Literally the size of matchsticks, these should be fine and even. They cook very quickly: useful for garnish – small piles of ingredients may be arranged Japanese style.

SHREDDED Cut into thin slices, then across into fine pieces. Firm cabbage and similar leaves may be shredded by cutting into chunks, then thinly slicing.

GRATED Use the coarse blade on a grater and discard the last, small chunk which cannot be processed.

CHOPPED Cut slices, thin sticks, then cut across to chop the ingredient. Halve and slice an onion, then cut across the slices so that they fall into small, reasonably even, pieces, but this is not as even as dicing. The pieces should be small unless roughly chopped, in which case they can be slightly larger and less even. Chop herbs by using a large sharp knife and a guillotine action.

DICED Cut into small, even cubes – about 5 mm/¼ in or slightly larger.

Shredded

In cubing and dicing, the food is first cut into slices and then in the opposite direction.

CUBED Cut larger cubes than required for dice – between 1 cm/½ in and 2.5 cm/1 in – but even in size.

CHUNKS Slightly larger than cubed and less even. No need to trim food into a neat square shape.

Marinating and macerating

These are both terms relating to soaking food before cooking or eating. Marinating is used for savoury foods and macerating is the term for soaking fruit before use in cooking or before eating.

There are two main reasons for soaking food – to impart flavours to it and to tenderize tough ingredients. Marinating meat in selected ingredients improves the texture as well as the flavour. Herbs, spices, fruit, wine and acids are all common ingredients for marinades. The ingredients may be mixed and used raw or liquids may be heated with flavourings, cooled and used as a marinade. The food may be soaked for anything from 30 minutes to three days, depending on the food and the required results.

When marinating for long periods, the food should be absolutely fresh – particularly meat and poultry. The food should always be covered and kept in a cool place; if left for longer than a couple of hours it must be placed in the refrigerator, particularly in warm weather. Turn and rearrange food during marinating to keep the ingredients evenly coated in the flavourings.

Stir frying techniques

Have all the ingredients prepared and ready for adding to the pan. Make sure that the diners are ready to eat too, as many stir fry dishes do not keep well once they have been cooked.

Heat the fat and add the ingredients that require longest cooking first. When they are part cooked, add the next batch of ingredients. Continue adding the ingredients in stages so that they are all cooked together when the dish is complete. In some cases, the additional ingredients may be mixed directly with the food in the pan, in others the part-cooked food should be pushed to one side and the new items stir fried quickly before all the food is combined.

TIMING STIR FRYING Giving exact timings for stir frying is difficult and can be misleading. The time necessary to cook food depends not only on the way it is cut and the heat of the pan, but on the volume of other ingredients, and the size of the cooking pan also plays a role. If the pan is full, the new ingredients take longer to cook; if a large, spacious pan is used the food has better contact with the base and it cooks more quickly.

With some commonsense and a bit of experience, you will soon recognize the right moment to add the next batch of ingredients. Take particular care to ensure that poultry is well cooked by checking the pieces at each cooking stage and before serving. If there are any signs of blood in the juices, the poultry is not cooked sufficiently.

STIR BRAISING This is similar to stir frying but with moisture in the pan, and it is often the natural follow-on technique after stir frying. Once the ingredients are stir fried, stock or other liquids are added and the cooking continues, with the ingredients being stirred, until the dish is complete and any sauce is reduced or thickened.

SERVING Lastly, remember that foods that are cooked quickly benefit from immediate serving, so transfer the food to a heated serving dish or indiviudal plates promptly. Have garnishes or accompaniments ready so that the complete course may be served at once. Remember that the wok or pan may be taken to the table and kept warm over a burner.

STIR FRYING FOR STARTERS

A stir fried first course can be light, colourful and thoroughly appetizing; perfect, in fact, for getting a meal off to good beginnings. Have all the ingredients organized, the pan on the hob (but not heated) and you can spring into action when guests have relaxed over pre-dinner drinks.

If the cooking time is especially short, remember to ensure everyone is sitting down – or at least making for the table – before you stir fry: better to have them waiting for a few minutes than to allow a splendid dish to cool and maybe spoil.

As well as the ideas in this chapter, many main course stir fried dishes are easily adapted to serving as starters by reducing the quantities of ingredients. Similarly, you can double up the amounts in these recipes to make a selection of delicious light lunches or suppers.

● Spicy Oriental Squid

When the pieces of squid are stir fried they curl to expose the diamond cuts. The choice of cooking oil is important to achieve a high temperature and satisfactory crisp results.

SERVES 4

12 squid, cleaned (see page 000)	2 garlic cloves, crushed
juice of 1 lemon	2 tsp sesame oil
1 green chilli, seeded and chopped	4 tbsp groundnut oil
¼ tsp five spice powder	1 red pepper, seeded and diced
	4 spring onions, thinly sliced
	4 tbsp soy sauce

The tentacles may be used or not as preferred. Slit the squid body sacs lengthways, then cut each into 2 – 3 pieces. Using a small, sharp pointed knife, score a zig-zag pattern on the inside of the pieces of squid. Do not cut right through the squid – simply mark a trellis pattern in the flesh.

Place the squid pieces in a basin. Add the lemon juice, chilli, five spice powder, garlic and sesame oil, and mix well to coat all the pieces in seasoning. Cover and leave to marinate for at least an hour – if possible leave the squid for 3 – 4 hours.

Heat the groundnut oil until shimmering, then stir fry the squid until browned. The pieces should curl to expose the attractive diamond cuts. Use a slotted spoon to remove the pieces from the pan and divide them between serving plates.

Pour off any excess oil from the pan, if necessary, leaving just enough to cook the vegetables. Stir fry the pepper and spring onions for 1 – 2 minutes, then sprinkle in the soy sauce and stir for a few seconds. Spoon the vegetable mixture and juices over the squid and serve at once.

Golden Baby Corn with Shrimps

SERVES 4

1 garlic clove, crushed
¼ tsp turmeric
2 tbsp light soy sauce
2 tbsp medium sherry
225 g/8 oz whole baby corn cobs
3 tbsp oil
1 celery stick, cut in short, fine strips
4 spring onions, shredded
¼ Iceberg lettuce, coarsely shredded
225 g/8 oz peeled and cooked shrimps or prawns
2 tsp grated lemon rind

Mix the garlic, turmeric, soy sauce and sherry in a large basin. Add the corn cobs and toss well to coat them in the seasonings. Cover and set aside for at least 30 minutes. The corn may be left to marinate for as long as several hours.

Heat 2 tablespoons of the oil and stir fry the celery for 30 seconds. Use a draining spoon to add the corn, reserving the juices. Stir fry the corn for 4 – 5 minutes. Mix in the spring onions and cook for 1 minute before stirring in the lettuce. Add the juices from the corn and stir fry for a further 30 – 60 seconds. The lettuce should still be crisp.

Divide the mixture between four warmed plates or dishes. Add the remaining oil to the pan. Stir fry the shrimps and lemon rind for 30 seconds, or until hot, then divide between the portions of corn. Serve at once.

COOK'S TIP

If using frozen shrimps or prawns in this, or any other recipe, remember to weigh them after thawing and draining.

Scallops with Avocado

This is a good way of stretching a few large scallops to serve four. Serve thin bread and butter or melba toast with this starter.

SERVES 4

1 lime
1 bunch watercress
2 avocados
large knob of butter
a little oil
8 large scallops, sliced
salt and white pepper

Cut a thin strip of rind from around the middle of the lime, then slice this across into very fine shreds. Quarter the lime and set it aside. Trim the stalks off the watercress.

Halve the avocado, discard the stone and cut the flesh into quarters. Remove the peel, then slice the avocado quarters and arrange the slices on serving plates.

Heat the butter with a little oil. Add the lime rind and cook for a few seconds. Add the scallops with the watercress and stir fry for 1 – 2 minutes, or until the scallops are just cooked. They are ready when just firm – overcook them and they become tough. Divide the scallops between the plates and add a wedge of lime to each portion. Serve at once – the lime juice may be squeezed over the scallops before they are eaten.

GOLDEN BABY CORN WITH SHRIMPS

Vegetable Snow Pancakes

Light pancakes made from egg whites and flavoured with spring onions are the ideal base on which to serve mixed vegetables. Large white radish or mooli, daikon in Japanese cuisine, peps up the already delicious broccoli and mushroom mixture.

SERVES 4

2 egg whites	225 g/8 oz broccoli
2 tbsp cornflour	225 g/8 oz mushrooms, thinly
salt	sliced
2 spring onions, finely chopped	2 tbsp soy sauce
	1 tbsp caster sugar
STIR FRIED VEGETABLES	1 tbsp rice vinegar or cider
5 cm/2 in piece white radish,	vinegar
peeled	oil for cooking
	2 tbsp sesame seeds

Lightly whisk the egg whites with 2 tablespoons water, adding the cornflour a teaspoonful at a time. Whisk in a little salt, then stir in the spring onions.

Cut the white radish lengthways into thin slices, then cut the slices into fine strips. Place these in a basin. Cut the broccoli into small pieces and mix them with the radish. Place the mushroom slices in a separate basin and add the soy sauce, sugar and vinegar. Mix well but try not to break up the mushroom slices. Cover and set the mixture aside.

The pancakes may be cooked individually in a wok or three to four at a time in a large frying pan. Heat a little oil, then lightly whisk the egg-white batter and pour a spoonful into the pan to make a thin round pancake. Cook until set and browned underneath, then turn and cook the second side until lightly browned. Drain the pancakes on absorbent kitchen paper and keep them hot. Make eight small pancakes.

Heat a little oil, then use a draining spoon to add the mushrooms. Stir fry over high heat for about 1 minute, until the mushrooms are browned. Add the radish and broccoli and continue cooking for about 3 minutes. Stir in the sesame seeds and cook for 1 minute, then pour in the juices from marinating the mushrooms.

Arrange the pancakes on individual plates, then top each with a portion of the stir fried vegetables. Serve the dish at once.

Aubergine Toppers

This is an interesting and unusual opening for a Mediterranean-style meal.

SERVES 4

1 large aubergine	1 small onion, halved and thinly sliced
salt and freshly ground black pepper	2 small white turnips, cut in fine strips
4 tomatoes, peeled and seeded	4 slices cooked ham, cut in fine strips
6 tbsp olive oil	4 basil sprigs, shredded
1 garlic clove, crushed	

Trim the aubergine and cut off a thin slice of peel, lengthways, from both sides. Cut the rest of the aubergine into four long slices. Place these in a colander and sprinkle with salt. Leave over a bowl for 20 minutes, then rinse and pat dry on absorbent kitchen paper. Cut the tomatoes into strips.

Heat 4 tablespoons of the oil and add the aubergine slices. Turn them after a few seconds, then cook until lightly browned. Turn the slices again to brown the second side. Transfer to serving plates and keep hot.

Heat the remaining oil. Add the garlic, onion and turnips, then stir fry the mixture for about 5 minutes, until the vegetables are cooked but still crunchy. Stir in the tomatoes, ham and seasoning, and cook the mixture for about 30 seconds.

Spoon the vegetable mixture over the aubergine slices and top each portion with shredded basil. Serve at once with some crusty bread to mop up the juices.

PEELING AND SEEDING TOMATOES

There are two ways of peeling tomatoes. The first is useful for firm fruit: spear a tomato on a metal fork, then hold it oiver a gas flame, turning the fork, until the skin blisters and bursts. Rub off the skin under cold water. When peeling a large quantity of tomatoes, place in a bowl and pour freshly boiling water over them. Leave the fruit for 30 – 60 seconds, the shorter time for very ripe tomatoes. Drain the tomatoes and slit their skins with the point of a knife – the skin should peel off easily.

To remove the seeds, halve a tomato, then use a small teaspoon to scoop out the seeds, leaving the shell and central part.

PEPPERAMA

Pepperama

This is a terrific summer starter – ideal for barbecues as you can heat the wok over the charcoal. It also makes a tempting side dish for kebabs or plain grilled meats.

SERVES 4

4 tbsp raisins
2 tbsp red wine
20 black olives, stoned and sliced
4 tbsp chopped fresh parsley
2 tsp grated lemon rind

4 large peppers, preferably red, green, yellow and orange
2 tbsp olive oil
3 tbsp pine kernels
salt and freshly ground black pepper

Heat the raisins and wine in a small saucepan until boiling, then set aside. Alternatively, place them in a small basin or suitable mug and cook in the microwave on full power for about 30 seconds, until hot. Mix the olives, parsley and lemon rind.

Halve the peppers lengthways, remove the core and all seeds, then slice the shells into thin strips. Heat the oil and stir fry the pine kernels for a minute or so, until they are just beginning to change colour. Add the pepper strips and continue to stir fry for 4 – 5 minutes. Stir in the raisins with their juices and add seasoning to taste. Cook for a few seconds, then spread out the peppers on individual plates or one large platter. Top with the olive mixture and serve.

Vegetable Cups with Tapenade

These stir fried vegetables in lettuce leaves are topped with tapenade to taste, then rolled up and eaten. The tapenade is highly seasoned to flavour the unsalted, stir fried vegetables. Do not overfill the lettuce leaves, and remember to provide large napkins or finger bowls for cleaning oily fingers.

SERVES 4

TAPENADE
175 g/6 oz black olives, stoned
50 g/2 oz can anchovy fillets
2 tbsp capers
1 large garlic clove, crushed
freshly ground black pepper
2 tbsp lemon juice
about ¼ cup/50 ml/4 fl oz olive oil

STIR FRY VEGETABLES
1 fennel bulb
4 celery sticks
2 tbsp olive oil
½ small onion, thinly sliced (a red onion gives the best flavour)
425 g/15 oz can artichoke hearts, drained
4 tbsp chopped fresh parsley
12 large Iceberg lettuce leaves to serve

The tapenade may be prepared well ahead as it keeps in a covered jar in the refrigerator for 2–3 days. Pound the olives to a paste in a mortar. Mash the anchovies with the oil from the can, then pound them into the olives. Gradually work in the capers and garlic to make a smooth paste. Add plenty of pepper and mix the lemon juice, then slowly work in the olive oil. Of course, the easiest way to make the paste is in a food processor or liquidizer; however, take care not to over-process the ingredients. Scrape all the tapenade into a small serving bowl and place it in the centre of a large platter.

Trim any browned ends off the fennel, then halve the bulb lengthways and cut it into fine slices. Thinly slice the celery. Heat the oil, then stir fry the fennel, celery and onion for 3 minutes. Add the artichoke hearts and stir fry for a further minute or so, until hot. Stir in the parsley.

Arrange the lettuce leaves on the platter around the bowl of tapenade. Divide the vegetables between the leaves and serve at once.

with the spring onions. Divide this salad between four serving plates.

Drain the oil from the cheese into a large pan and heat it until quite hot – olive oil overheats quickly so this does not take long over medium to high heat. Turn the cheese into the pan and stir fry it until golden brown. Add the grapes and toss them with the cheese for a few seconds simply to warm them slightly.

Spoon the halloumi and grapes on the prepared salads and serve at once, with crusty bread to savour the cooking juices.

HALLOUMI WITH GRAPES

Halloumi with Grapes

Halloumi is a tough sheeps' milk cheese of the Middle East, Turkey and Greece. Often served barbecued, the cheese forms a crisp crust on cooking and the middle softens to a pleasing texture. Serve this starter piping hot – the sweet, crisp grapes contrast deliciously with the cheese.

SERVES 4

350 g/12 oz halloumi cheese	2 tbsp coarsely crushed coriander seeds
4 tbsp olive oil	freshly ground black pepper
1 tsp dried oregano	225 g/8 oz seedless green grapes
1 tsp fresh thyme leaves	1 bunch watercress
	2 spring onions, chopped

Cut the cheese into 1–2.5 cm/½–1 in cubes and place in a basin. Add the olive oil, oregano, thyme, coriander and a good sprinkling of black pepper. Mix well, cover and set aside to marinate for at least an hour – the cheese may be left overnight in the refrigerator.

Remove all stalks from the grapes, then wash and dry them. Trim the leaves off the watercress and mix them

Mushroom Feast

Equally good for a light lunch as for an appetizer, sun-dried tomatoes enrich stir fried mixed mushrooms.

SERVES 4

25 g/1 oz dried boletus mushrooms or ceps	225 g/8 oz chestnut mushrooms, sliced
4 sun-dried tomatoes	2 tbsp olive oil
2 tbsp port	large knob of butter
225 g/8 oz oyster mushrooms	4 tbsp snipped chives
	4 tbsp chopped fresh parsley

Place the dried mushrooms in a small saucepan with the tomatoes. Add just enough water to cover, then bring to the boil. Reduce the heat and simmer, uncovered, for 15 minutes. Drain, reserving the cooking liquor. Slice the mushrooms if necessary.

Dice the tomatoes, then mix the tomatoes and port and set aside. Strain the reserved mushroom cooking liquor through scalded muslin back into the pan. Boil the liquid until it is reduced to about 2 tablespoons, then pour it over the tomatoes.

Trim any tough stalks from the oyster mushrooms. Heat the oil and butter, then stir fry the chestnut mushrooms and dried mushrooms over high heat for 1 minute. Add the oyster mushrooms and stir fry for about 2 minutes, until hot but not softened. Stir in the tomatoes with their liquid, then boil the mixture rapidly for about 30 seconds.

Finally, toss the herbs into the pan and serve the mushrooms at once, piled in individual dishes. Serve warmed crusty bread to absorb the juices.

Hot Chicken Liver Salad

This is equally good as a light lunch or for supper.

SERVES 4

225 g/8 oz chicken livers
½ tsp ground coriander
¼ tsp ground mace
¼ tsp paprika
1 tbsp plain flour
salt and freshly ground black
   pepper

2 spring onions, chopped
4 tbsp chopped fresh parsley
1 tsp grated lemon rind
225 g/8 oz rindless bacon rashers,
   diced
2 tbsp olive oil
salad of mixed leaves to serve
lemon wedges to garnish

Rinse, drain and dry the chicken livers on absorbent kitchen paper. Trim any membranes from them, then halve or quarter each piece of liver. Sprinkle the coriander, mace, paprika, flour and plenty of seasoning over the livers and mix well to coat all the pieces.

Mix the spring onion with the parsley and lemon rind, then set aside. Prepare the salad bases for serving the chicken livers.

Place the bacon in a cold pan and stir fry over medium to high heat until the fat from the bacon runs.

Continue to stir fry until all the bacon pieces have become browned and are crisp. Use a slotted spoon to remove them from the pan and then drain the pieces on absorbent kitchen paper.

Add the olive oil to the fat remaining in the pan, heat it briefly, then add the chicken livers with all their seasonings. Stir fry until firm, lightly browned and cooked – which should take about 5 minutes. Mix in the crispy bacon and the spring onion mixture. Spoon the chicken livers onto the prepared salads. Garnish the dish with lemon wedges for their juice and serve it at once, with melba toast.

TO MAKE MELBA TOAST

Lightly toast medium-thick bread slices on both sides. Cut off the crusts and slice each piece through horizontally to give two very thin slices. Toast the uncooked sides of the bread well away from the heat source until lightly browned and slightly curled. Cool on a wire rack.

SIMPLY DELICIOUS MAIN DISHES

*This chapter is full of ideas for everyday main meals,
suitable for the family or informal suppers with
friends. They are inexpensive, easy and satisfying,
so guaranteed to become firm favourites. There are
ideas for fish and seafood (ideal for adapting to
favourite fillets or steaks), quick and easy options for
poultry, and interesting ways with sausages or offal.*

*Flip the stir fries out on to dishes of cooked rice,
pasta or salad; roll them in hot cooked pancakes;
spoon them into pitta bread or slit French bread; or
pile them into steaming-hot baked potatoes. In fact,
treat these dishes as you would any familiar main
dish and, when time is short, simply serve up chunks
of crusty bread and a crunchy side salad to complete
the meal.*

● Lemon Fish Strips with Courgettes

SERVES 4

675 g/½ lb whiting fillets or other
   firm white fish fillets, skinned
salt and freshly ground black
   pepper
3 tbsp plain flour
grated rind of 1 lemon
3 tbsp oil

½ small onion, thinly sliced and
   separated into strips
1 red pepper, cut in thin strips
225 g/8 oz small courgettes,
   trimmed, halved lengthways
   and cut in 5 cm/2 in long sticks
4 tbsp snipped chives
lemon wedges to garnish

Cut the fish fillets across into 1 cm/½ in wide strips.
Place them in a dish, then sprinkle with the seasoning,
flour and lemon rind. Mix well to coat all the fish evenly.

   Heat the oil, then stir fry the onion and pepper for 3
minutes, until lightly cooked, before adding the fish.
Carefully stir fry the fish, taking care not to break the
strips, for 4 – 5 minutes, until lightly browned. Use a
slotted spoon to transfer the fish mixture to a heated
serving dish.

   Add the courgettes to the oil remaining in the pan
(there should be just enough to keep the pan greased)
and stir fry them over high heat for about 2 minutes, so
that they are hot and slightly tender. Stir in the chives,
then arrange the courgettes around the fish. Garnish
with lemon wedges and serve at once. The juice from
the lemon should be squeezed over the fish before the
fish is eaten.

COOK'S TIP

Snipped chives are cut into small pieces using scissors. Hold the washed bunch firmly in one hand and
snip off the ends into a basin.

Mackerel with Gooseberries

Tart gooseberries are a traditional accompaniment for rich, full-flavoured mackerel; however, they are not usually stir fried together. Serve this summery combination with new potatoes and fresh peas or crisp French beans.

SERVES 4

4 small to medium mackerel, gutted with heads and tails off
salt and freshly ground black pepper
4 tbsp plain flour
knob of butter
1 small onion, halved and thinly sliced

225 g/8 oz gooseberries, topped and tailed
50 g/2 oz light soft brown sugar
3 tbsp oil
2 tbsp chopped fresh dill or fennel
dill or fennel sprigs to garnish

Lay the mackerel one by one on a board, skin side uppermost, then run your thumb firmly along the length of the backbone. Turn the fish over and lift off the bone, starting from the tail end. The loosened backbone should lift off easily, taking the majority of the other bones with it. Pick off any remaining bones, then cut the fish across into 1 cm/½ in wide strips. Coat the fish with plenty of seasoning and the flour.

Melt the butter and stir fry the onion for about 5 minutes, until lightly cooked. Add the gooseberries and continue to stir fry for about 3 – 4 minutes, until the fruit is lightly cooked. Add the sugar and stir fry until it melts, combining with the fruit juices in a tangy glaze. Spoon the fruit around the edge of a serving dish and keep hot.

Wipe the pan with absorbent kitchen paper. Heat the oil and stir fry the fish strips over medium to high heat until golden and slightly crisp at the edges. Drain the strips on absorbent kitchen paper and toss the dill or fennel with them. Arrange the fish on the serving dish with the gooseberry sauce. Garnish with dill or fennel sprigs and serve at once.

Fish with Black Beans

Serve this flavoursome Oriental-style fish dish with plain cooked rice. If it is included along with several other dishes as part of an extensive menu, the quantity of fish may be reduced by half.

SERVES 4

900 g/2 lb plaice, whiting or haddock fillet, skinned
2 tbsp salted black beans
4 tbsp dry sherry
2 tbsp light soy sauce
1 tsp sesame oil
3 tbsp cornflour
2 tbsp oil

5 cm/2 in piece fresh root ginger, peeled and cut in fine strips
1 green chilli, seedeed and cut into rings
1 garlic clove, crushed
1 piece lemon grass or strip of lemon rind
1 bunch spring onions, cut diagonally into strips

Cut the fish across into 1 cm/½ in wide strips and place these in a large shallow dish. Sprinkle the salted black beans, sherry, soy sauce and sesame oil over the fish. Cover the dish and leave the strips to marinate for 2 – 3 hours.

When you are ready to cook the fish, drain the strips well, reserving all the juices. Toss the strips in the cornflour.

Heat the oil, then stir fry the ginger, chilli, garlic and lemon grass or rind over medium heat for 4 – 5 minutes, to extract their flavour. Add the fish strips to the pan and stir fry them carefully, avoiding breaking the strips, until they are lightly browned.

Add all the spring onions and continue to stir fry for 2 minutes, until the onions are cooked. Add 4 tablespoons water to the reserved marinating juices and pour them into the pan. Bring to the boil over high heat, reduce the heat and stir fry for 1 minute, then serve at once.

FISH WITH BLACK BEANS

Cod with French-Style Peas

Fresh peas make this a special dish, in which case it is worth substituting chunks of monkfish for the cod; for a homely, mid-week meal opt for frozen peas and less expensive white fish. Rice, pasta, boiled or baked potatoes are all suitable accompaniments.

SERVES 4

675 g/1½ lb thick cod fillet, skinned and cut in chunks
salt and freshly ground black pepper
1 tbsp lemon juice
2 tbsp olive oil
knob of butter
1 large onion, chopped

1 garlic clove, crushed
225 g/8 oz shelled fresh peas, blanched until just tender, or frozen peas
1 Cos lettuce heart, shredded
1 tbsp chopped fresh dill or fennel
2 tbsp chopped fresh parsley
lemon or lime wedges to serve

Place the fish on a plate, season it well and sprinkle with the lemon juice. Heat the oil and butter together until the butter melts, then stir fry the onion and garlic for 5 minutes, until the onion is just beginning to soften.

Stir in the peas and stir fry them with the onion for a further 5 minutes before adding the lettuce. Continue to stir fry the vegetable mixture for 2 minutes, until the lettuce is wilted. Add the fish, dill or fennel and parsley, then stir fry gently for a further 5 minutes or until the pieces of fish are just firm. Taste and adjust the seasoning before serving with wedges of lime or lemon for their juice.

COD WITH FRENCH-STYLE PEAS

SPICY PRAWNS WITH   OMELETTE

Spicy Prawns with Omelette

SERVES 4

1 green chilli, seeded and finely sliced
2 garlic cloves, crushed
2.5 cm/1 in piece fresh root ginger, grated
½ tsp turmeric
pinch of ground cloves
1 tbsp ground coriander
1 tbsp ground cumin
juice of 2 limes
salt and pepper

450 g/1 lb peeled cooked prawns
4 tbsp oil
1 large onion, thinly sliced
3 tbsp chopped salted peanuts
100 ml/4 fl oz coconut milk
2 tbsp chopped fresh coriander

OMELETTE

2 eggs, beaten
½ tsp sesame oil
1 tsp oil

In a large dish, mix the chilli, garlic, ginger, turmeric, cloves, coriander and cumin with the lime juice and plenty of seasoning. Add the prawns and mix well to coat them all in the sauce, then cover and set aside to marinate for 2 – 3 hours. Heat the oil and stir fry the onion until it is just beginning to brown – about 10 minutes. Add the prawns with all the marinating spices and stir fry for 5 minutes to cook the spices. Add the peanuts and coconut milk and stir until the mixture is just boiling. Taste and adjust the seasoning, then transfer to a serving dish and sprinkle with the coriander.

You will need a large flat pan for making the omelette. Beat the eggs with 2 tablespoons water and the sesame oil, adding a little seasoning. Heat the oil, pour in the eggs and cook over high heat until set and brown underneath. Use a large slice to flip the omelette over and cook the second side until browned. Cut the omelette into strips and arrange it in a criss-cross pattern on the prawns. Serve at once.

COOK'S TIP

If you lack the confidence to flip the omelette using a slice, slide it out on to a plate, then invert it back into the pan to cook the second side.

Squid Provençal

SERVES 4

8 medium squid
4 tbsp plain flour
salt and freshly ground black
  pepper
6 tbsp olive oil
1 onion, halved and sliced
1 green pepper, thinly sliced
1–2 garlic cloves, crushed
1 bay leaf
450 g/1 lb ripe tomatoes, peeled
  and quartered
50 g/2 oz stoned black olives,
  sliced
4 tbsp chopped fresh parsley

First clean the squid (see below). Slice the body sac into rings and cut up the tentacles, if using, into small pieces. Dry the prepared squid on absorbent kitchen paper, then place the pieces in a basin.

Sprinkle the flour and plenty of seasoning over the squid. Heat the oil and stir fry the squid briskly until lightly browned. Use a slotted spoon to remove the pieces from the pan and drain them on absorbent kitchen paper.

Add the onion, pepper, garlic and bay leaf to the oil remaining in the pan. Stir fry these ingredients until the onion and pepper are slightly softened – about 5 minutes. Add the tomatoes and continue cooking, stirring all the time, for a further 5 minutes, until the tomatoes are soft but not pulpy. Add seasoning to taste and the olives, then replace the squid in the pan. Sprinkle in the parsley and stir over high heat for a minute or so. Serve with rice or plenty of crusty bread.

TO CLEAN SQUID

Pull the tentacles and head out of the body sac and it will bring with it all the innards which should be discarded. The tentacles may be cooked if liked, in which case they should be cut off just above the eyes. Discard the rest of the head. Pull out the transparent quill which is inside the body sac. Rinse the sac inside and out under cold water and rub off the mottled skin. Rinse the tentacles if using. Drain well.

LEMON MARMALADE CHICKEN

Chicken with Broccoli and Cashew Nuts

SERVES 4

1 tbsp cornflour	2 large boneless chicken breasts, skinned and cut into thin strips
4 tbsp dry sherry	50 g/2 oz unsalted cashew nuts
4 tbsp soy sauce	225 g/8 oz broccoli florets, broken into small pieces
100 ml/4 fl oz chicken stock	200 g/7 oz can bamboo shoots, drained and sliced
1 tsp sesame oil	6 spring onions, sliced diagonally
2 tbsp sunflower or groundnut oil	

Blend the cornflour to a smooth thin paste with the sherry, soy sauce and stock, then set the mixture aside.

Heat the sesame and sunflower or groundnut oil, then stir fry the chicken and cashew nuts until the chicken has become golden and cooked, and the nuts have been lightly browned.

Add the broccoli, bamboo shoots and spring onions and continue to stir fry for 3 – 4 minutes, until the broccoli is lightly cooked.

Give the cornflour mixture a stir, then pour it into the pan and stir over medium heat until the sauce boils. Allow the mixture to boil for a minute or so, stirring all the time, so that all the ingredients are coated in a lightly thickened sauce. Serve at once.

Lemon Marmalade Chicken

This zesty chicken dish is extremely simple and it tastes terrific with new potatoes and a crisp salad.

SERVES 4

4 boneless chicken breasts, skinned	1 thyme sprig
2 tbsp plain flour	grated rind and juice of 1 large lemon
salt and freshly ground black pepper	4 tbsp lemon marmalade
1 tbsp sunflower oil	**GARNISH (OPTIONAL)**
50 g/2 oz butter	lemon slices
1 bay leaf	thyme sprigs

Slice the chicken breasts across into large medallions, then toss the pieces in the flour and plenty of seasoning.

Heat the oil and half the butter, then stir fry the bay leaf, thyme and chicken until golden and cooked through. Add the lemon rind and juice and continue cooking, stirring all the time, for about 30 seconds to coat all the chicken with lemon.

Next add the marmalade with 2 tablespoons water and stir until the marmalade has dissolved, and has combined with the other ingredients to form a bubbling glaze. Stir in the remaining butter to give the glaze a good gloss and to enrich the dish. Serve at once, garnished with lemon slices and thyme, if wished.

CHICKEN WITH BROCCOLI AND CASHEW NUTS

TURKEY WITH CHESTNUTS AND SPROUTS

Turkey with Chestnuts and Sprouts

Chestnuts canned in brine may be substituted for the fresh ones in this recipe.

SERVES 4

450 g/1 lb chestnuts	2 tbsp oil
675 g/1½ lb Brussels sprouts	1 onion, chopped
450 g/1 lb skinned fillet of turkey breast, cubed	2 large sage sprigs
3 tbsp plain flour	1 thyme sprig
salt and pepper	250 m/8 fl oz chicken or turkey stock
	100 m/4 fl oz medium cider

Wash the chestnuts, then use a pointed knife to make a slit in each one. Place in a saucepan, cover with water and bring to the boil. Reduce the heat and simmer for 15 minutes. Drain and remove the chestnut shells.

Halve any large Brussels sprouts, then blanch the vegetables in boiling water for 2 minutes. Drain and set aside.

Toss the turkey with the flour and seasoning. Heat the oil, then stir fry the onion, sage and thyme for about 7 minutes, until the onion is softened. Add the turkey and continue to stir fry until all the pieces are golden and cooked. Stir in the chestnuts and Brussels sprouts, then continue to cook for 5 minutes before pouring in the stock and cider.

Stir the mixture until it boils, then stir over medium heat for 2 minutes, until the juices are thickened. Taste for seasoning before serving.

Chicken with Sweetcorn and Almonds

SERVES 4

3 boneless chicken breasts, skinned and cut into 2.5 cm/1 in chunks	50 g/2 oz whole blanched almonds
2 tbsp cornflour	6 spring onions, sliced diagonally
1 egg white	3 tbsp soy sauce
1 tsp sesame oil	2 tbsp lemon juice
2 tbsp oil	4 tbsp ginger wine
	200 g/7 oz can sweetcorn

Place the chicken pieces in a basin. Add the cornflour and mix well to coat all the chicken. Lightly whisk the egg white, then add it to the chicken with the sesame oil and mix well.

Heat the oil and stir fry the almonds until golden. Use a slotted spoon to remove the nuts from the pan and drain them on absorbent kitchen paper. Give the chicken mixture a stir, then tip it all into the oil remaining in the pan. Stir fry briskly until all the pieces are golden brown and cooked through.

Add the spring onions and continue to stir fry for 2 minutes before pouring in the soy sauce, lemon juice and ginger wine. Stir in the sweetcorn and stir fry for 2 minutes, until the mixture is hot and glazed with cooking juices. Toss in the almonds and serve at once.

Spicy Mince with Peas

Serve this quick mince dish and its cucumber raita topping with fragrant pillau rice or hot nan bread.

SERVES 4

450 g/1 lb minced lamb	1 cinnamon stick
2 tbsp ground coriander	1 tbsp cumin seeds
1 tsp ground ginger	1 tbsp mustard seeds
6 green cardamoms	1 large potato, diced
2 bay leaves	100 g/4 oz frozen peas
juice of 1 lemon	50 g/2 oz raisins
salt and freshly ground black pepper	
	TOPPING
2 tbsp oil	¼ cucumber, peeled and diced
1 onion, chopped	100 ml/4 fl oz natural yogurt
2 garlic cloves, crushed	1 tbsp chopped fresh mint
	mint sprigs to garnish (optional)

SPICY MINCE WITH PEAS

Place the lamb in a basin with the coriander, ginger, cardamoms, bay leaves and lemon juice. Add seasoning and mix thoroughly. If possible, cover and leave to marinate for several hours or even overnight in the refrigerator.

Heat the oil, then stir fry the onion, garlic, cinnamon, cumin, mustard and potato until the potato dice are browned all over. Make sure that the pan does not overheat or the spices will burn. Add the mince mixture and continue to stir fry until the meat is browned. Stir in the peas and raisins, and then cook for a further 5 minutes. Taste for seasoning, then transfer to a heated serving dish.

For the topping, mix the cucumber and yogurt with the chopped mint, then swirl this through the spicy mince. Garnish the dish with fresh mint, if wished, and serve at once.

Mince Creole

SERVES 4

225 g/8 oz long-grain rice	2 garlic cloves, crushed
salt and freshly ground black peper	450 g/1 lb minced steak
2 tbsp oil	1 tbsp chilli powder
1 large onion, thinly sliced	2 × 425 g/15 oz cans chopped tomatoes
1 green pepper, seeded and sliced	
	GARNISH
1 red pepper, seeded and sliced	4 tomatoes, peeled and diced
	3 tbsp chopped fresh parsley

Cook the rice by adding it to a saucepan of boiling salted water. Bring the water back to the boil, then reduce the heat slightly and cover the pan. Simmer the rice for 15 – 20 minutes, or until tender.

Meanwhile, heat the oil and stir fry the onion, peppers and garlic for 5 minutes. Push them to one side of the pan and add the steak. Stir fry the meat briskly in the middle of the pan until evenly browned and well cooked. Add the chilli and plenty of seasoning, then mix in the peppers and onion and continue to cook for 2 – 3 minutes. Pour in the tomatoes and bring the mixture to the boil, stirring all the time. Continue to cook, stirring, over medium heat for 5 – 7 minutes.

Drain the rice and transfer it to a serving dish. Ladle the mince mixture over the rice, then arrange the diced tomatoes and chopped parsley on top. Serve at once.

Sweet-Sour Pork Balls

SERVES 4

450 g/1 lb minced pork
1 tsp sesame oil
4 tbsp cornflour
1 egg
2 tbsp soy sauce
2 tbsp oil

SWEET AND SOUR SAUCE

1 tsp cornflour
4 tbsp dry sherry

4 tbsp soy sauce
3 tbsp tomato purée
4 tbsp demerara sugar
2 tbsp white wine vinegar
225 g/8 oz can pineapple chunks
    in syrup
1 large onion, cut in chunks
1 large green pepper, cut in
    chunks
2 carrots, cut in 2.5 c/1 in strips

Pound the pork with the sesame oil until well mixed, then mix in the cornflour, egg and soy sauce in the same way. Have a plate ready to hold the pork balls. Wash, then wet your hands under cold water. Take small portions of the meat mixture, about the size of walnuts, and knead them into balls. Keep wetting your hands as this prevents the meat from sticking to them, and it gives the balls an even surface.

Before cooking the pork balls, start preparing the sauce: blend the cornflour to a paste with 4 tablespoons water. Add the sherry and soy sauce, then stir in the tomato purée, sugar and vinegar. Drain the liquid from the pineapple into the mixture.

Heat the oil and stir fry the pork balls until evenly browned and cooked through. Use a draining spoon to remove them from the pan.

Add the onion, pepper and carrots to the hot fat and stir fry these ingredients for about 5 minutes, until slightly softened. Give the liquid sauce mixture a stir, then pour it into the pan and bring to the boil, stirring all the time. Stir in the pork balls and pineapple and cook, stirring over reduced heat for 3 – 4 minutes. Serve with rice.

● Satay-flavour Pork

SERVES 4

450 g/1 lb lean boneless pork, cut in thin strips
2 tbsp lime or lemon juice
2 tbsp ground coriander
1 tsp ground ginger
1 garlic clove, crushed
salt and freshly ground black pepper
1 tsp sesame oil
4 tbsp groundnut oil
1 bunch spring onions, shredded

SAUCE

1 small onion, chopped
2 garlic cloves, crushed
juice of 1 lime or lemon
½ tsp chilli powder
4 tbsp tahini
4 tbsp crunchy peanut butter
2 tbsp soy sauce

SALAD

½ Iceberg lettuce, shredded
½ cucumber, halved and thinly sliced

GARNISH

spring onion curls
lime or lemon wedges

Place the pork in a basin. Add the lime or lemon juice, coriander, ginger, garlic, seasoning and sesame oil. Stir well so that all the pieces of meat are coated in the seasoning mix. Cover and leave to marinate for several hours or overnight.

For the sauce, blend the onion, garlic, lime or lemon juice, chilli and tahini to a paste in a luquidizer or food processor. Stir 3 – 4 tablespoons boiling water into the peanut butter to soften it to a paste, then stir in the blended mixture and the soy sauce. Add a little extra boiling water if necessary to thin the sauce.

Arrange the lettuce and cucumber on a platter or individual plates. Add the spring onion curls. Heat the groundnut oil and stir fry the pork until browned and cooked through. Add the spring onions and stir fry for another minute. Arrange the meat on the salad base.

Spoon a little peanut sauce over the meat and spring onions, then serve the rest separately. Add lime wedges to garnish and serve at once.

COOK'S TIP

Tahini is a beige-coloured paste made from sesame seeds. Available from wholefood shops and oriental stores.

Pork with Orange

Pasta, rice or buckwheat are excellent accompaniments to this dish. Alternatively, the pork may be piled into slit baked potatoes, rolled in pancakes or served in taco shells.

SERVES 4

450 g/1 lb lean boneless pork
3 sage sprigs
grated rind and juice of 1 orange
2 tbsp plain flour
salt and freshly ground black
    pepper
2 tbsp oil
1 onion, halved and thinly sliced
225 g/8 oz carrots, cut into fine
    strips
1 tbsp clear honey
2 tbsp dry sherry

Cut the pork across the grain into thin slices, then cut the slices into strips. Place the meat in a basin. Discard any thick stalks from the sage, then finely shred the sprigs (the easiest way to do this is to snip them with scissors) and add them to the pork with the orange rind and juice. Mix well, then cover and leave to marinate for at least two hours. The meat may be marinated and chilled for up to 24 hours.

Use a draining spoon to remove the meat from the orange juice, pressing the strips against the side of the basin to squeeze out as much liquid as possible. Transfer the meat to a plate or clean basin, then sprinkle the flour and plenty of seasoning over it. Mix lightly to coat the strips.

Heat the oil, then stir fry the onion and carrots for 3 – 4 minutes. Add the meat and continue stir frying until the strips are evenly browned and cooked. Pour in the reserved marinating juices, the honey and sherry. Stir the mixture, until the juices boil and thicken slightly to coat the pork and vegetables in a shiny glaze. Serve the dish at once.

Chilli Pork with Peanuts and Peaches

Good with rice, baked potatoes or in taco shells, this spicy pork and peanut mixture may be hotted up by adding extra chilli, or cooled by cutting it down to a mere pinch.

SERVES 4

450 g/1 lb lean boneless pork, cut
    into thin strips
1 tsp chilli powder
1 tsp ground allspice
2 cloves garlic, crushed
2tsp sesame oil
2 tbsp oil
1 onion, thinly sliced
50 g/2 oz roasted peanuts
225 g/8 oz French beans, lightly
    cooked
425 g/15 oz can peach slices,
    drained
salt and freshly ground black
    pepper
250 ml/8 fl oz soured cream to
    serve

Place the pork in a dish, then mix in the chilli, allspice, garlic and sesame oil. Cover and leave to marinate for at least 2 hours or overnight in the refrigerator.

Heat the oil and stir fry the onion for 5 minutes before adding the pork. Stir fry the meat until lightly browned all over. Add the peanuts and cook for a further 2 minutes before mixing in the beans and peaches. Continue cooking for about 5 minutes, so that the beans and peaches are piping hot and the pork cooked through. Add seasoning to taste, then serve at once, offering soured cream with the spicy pork.

CHILLI PORK WITH PEANUTS AND PEACHES

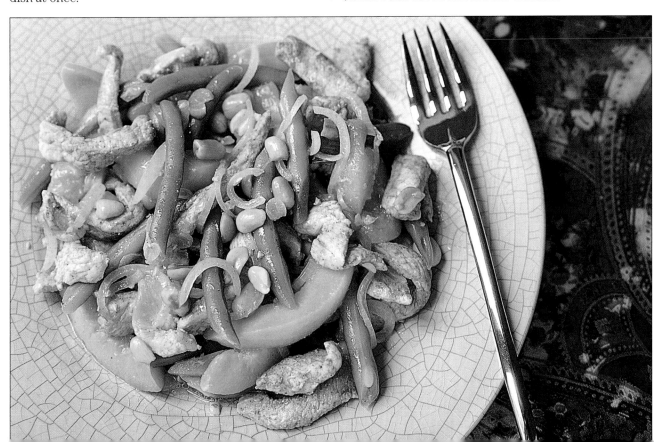

Pork with Sweet Potato

This recipe is under the influence of, rather than authentic to, Caribbean cooking. I hope you like the slightly off-beat combination of the cooking method and ingredients. It's good served very simply with a refreshing salad of finely shredded celery, cucumber, spring onions and pineapple, and some crusty bread; alternatively, cook up a pot of rice and red beans to make a really hearty meal.

SERVES 4

1 large sweet potato, scrubbed
450 g/1 lb lean boneless pork, finely diced
2 tsp ground cinnamon
freshly grated nutmeg
pinch of ground cloves or 3 whole cloves
1 garlic clove, crushed
3 thyme sprigs

grated rind and juice of 1 lime
salt and pepper
4 tbsp groundnut oil
2 green chillies, seeded and chopped
1 pepper, seeded and diced
1 onion, thinly sliced
25 g/1 oz raisins
6 tomatoes, peeled and roughly chopped

Cook the sweet potato in a saucepan of boiling water for 20 minutes, or until almost tender (it must not be too soft or it will break up when stir fried with the meat). Drain and cool the potato under cold water, then peel and cut it into cubes (about 2.5 cm/1 in).

Meanwhile, place the pork in a basin. Add the cinnamon, a good sprinkling of nutmeg, the cloves, garlic, thyme, lime rind and juice. Add some seasoning, then mix all the flavourings with the meat. If time allows, cover and set the meat aside to marinate for a couple of hours.

Heat the oil, then stir fry the meat with all the seasonings over fairly high heat until well browned. Use a slotted spoon to remove the meat from the pan. Add the chillies, pepper and onion to the oil remaining in the pan. Stir fry the vegetables over medium heat for 5 – 7 minutes, until they are beginning to soften. Add the cubes of sweet potato and continue stir frying, taking care not to break the potato, until all the sweet potato cubes are tender and thoroughly hot.

Stir in the raisins and tomatoes, replace the meat in the pan and mix well. Moisten the mixture with 4 tablespoons water and continue stir frying, adding a little more water to keep the mixture juicy, but not wet. The pork should be piping hot, the raisins plump and the tomatoes pulpy, but the sweet potato should still be (just) holding its shape. Taste and adjust the seasoning before serving.

TO COOK BUCKWHEAT

Roasted buckwheat has a nutty taste. To serve 4, place 175 g/6 oz buckwheat in a saucepan and pour in 500 ml/16 fl oz water. Add a little salt, then bring to the boil. Cover the pan tightly, reduce the heat to the lowest setting and leave 30 minutes. Fork up the grains and serve.

PORK WITH SAUERKRAUT

Pork with Sauerkraut

Simple, yet tasty, serve this stir fry with boiled or baked potatoes or cooked buckwheat.

SERVES 4

450 g/1 lb lean boneless pork, diced	1 onion, chopped
1 tsp paprika	1 bay leaf
1 garlic clove, crushed	1 large sage sprig
1 tbsp caraway seeds (optional)	2 full-flavoured eating apples, peeled, cored and diced
salt and freshly ground black pepper	450 g/1 lb sauerkraut, well drained and shredded
3 tbsp oil	100 ml/4 fl oz soured cream or Greek-style yogurt

Mix the pork, paprika, garlic, caraway (if used) and seasoning so that all the meat is well coated in the flavouring ingredients. The meat benefits from being left to marinate for a few hours (or overnight in the refrigerator), but this is not essential.

Heat the oil, then stir fry the onion, bay leaf and sage for 3 minutes. Add the pork with all the seasoning and stir fry over fairly high heat for 5 minutes. Add the apples, then continue to stir fry until the pork is well cooked and browned. Add the sauerkraut and stir fry for a few minutes to heat the vegetable through.

When the sauerkraut is piping hot, stir in the soured cream or yogurt to moisten the mixture. Taste and adjust the seasoning and stir for a few seconds, but do not overcook as the cream or yogurt will curdle.

Smoked Sausage Succotash

This is a quick variation of the American stew of beans and sweetcorn.

SERVES 4

knob of butter	2 × 425 g/15 oz cans butter beans
1 small onion, finely chopped	3 ripe tomatoes, peeled, seeded and diced
350 g/12 oz smoked pork sausage, sliced	150 ml/¼ pint single cream
225 g/8 oz frozen sweetcorn	salt and pepper
	2 tbsp chopped fresh parsley

Melt the butter, then stir fry the onion and sausage together until the sausage is lightly browned and succulent, and the onion softened – about 8 minutes.

Add the sweetcorn and butter beans. Continue stir frying for 5 minutes, or until the corn is thawed and cooked. Lastly stir in the tomatoes and cook for 1 minute before pouring in the cream and adding a little seasoning. Heat gently but do not allow to boil or the cream will curdle. Taste for seasoning, then sprinkle in the parsley and serve.

SAUSAGE STIR-ABOUT

Sausage Stir-About

This tasty mixture is good in baked potatoes, taco shells, rolled in pancakes or stuffed into warmed split pitta bread. The dish can be topped with natural yogurt or soured cream if you like.

SERVES 4

225 g/8 oz pork sausagemeat
50 g/2 oz fresh breadcrumbs
1 onion, grated
50 g/2 oz ready-to-eat dried apricots, chopped
1 tsp dried marjoram or oregano
salt and pepper
4 tbsp oil
450 g/1 lb potatoes, diced
225 g/8 oz cut green beans or broad beans, cooked until just tender
lots of chopped fresh parsley

Mix the sausagemeat, breadcrumbs, onion, apricots, marjoram or oregano and seasoning until thoroughly combined. Use two spoons to separate the mixture into small lumps about the size of walnuts – there is no need to be too fussy about shape as the meat will break up during cooking.

Heat the oil and stir fry the potatoes until they are crisp and golden brown, controlling the heat carefully to prevent the oil from overheating. Add the lumps of sausagemeat and continue stir frying over medium heat until all the meat is well cooked. Add the beans and stir fry for 3 – 5 minutes, until they are piping hot. Sprinkle in lots of parsley and serve at once.

Chilli Franks

A quick, tasty dish to serve with rice or baked potatoes. Use good-quality frankfurters for best results, and adjust the number of chillies according to personal preference and their type – if using mild chillies, then add four; if using very hot ones, then two will be sufficient.

SERVES 4

2 tbsp oil
1 large onion, chopped
2 garlic cloves, crushed
2 – 4 green chillies, seeded and chopped
1 green pepper, seeded and chopped
8 – 12 frankfurters (depending on size), sliced
1 tbsp ground cumin
1 tbsp dried marjoram
salt and pepper
2 × 425 g/15 oz cans red kidney beans, drained
2 × 425 g/15 oz cans chopped tomatoes

Heat the oil, then stir fry the onion, garlic, chillies and pepper for 4 – 5 minutes, until softened slightly. Add the frankfurters and continue to stir fry for about 10 minutes, or until the sausage slices are browned.

Stir in the cumin, marjoram and seasoning, and cook for 1 minute before tipping in the kidney beans and tomatoes. Stir well and bring to the boil, then simmer the mixture for 3 minutes, continuing to stir all the time, before serving.

GAMMON WITH CAULIFLOWER

Gammon with Cauliflower

A good recipe for inexpensive gammon offcuts or for corner gammon.

SERVES 4

1 small cauliflower, trimmed and broken into small florets
450 g/1 lb gammon, trimmed and cut into large dice
2 tbsp plain flour
freshly ground black pepper
1 tbsp fennel seeds (optional)
2 tbsp oil
1 large onion, chopped
1 bay leaf
2 large sage sprigs
250 ml/8 fl oz unsweetened apple juice

Plunge the cauliflower into a large saucepan of boiling water. Bring the water back to the boil, cook for 1 minute, then drain the florets and set them aside.

Toss the gammon with the flour, plenty of pepper and the fennel seeds, if using. Heat the oil, add the gammon and any loose flour. Stir fry for 1 minute, then add the onion, bay leaf and sage. Continue to cook until the diced gamon is evenly browned and cooked through. Add the cauliflower and stir fry for a further 3 minutes.

Pour in the apple juice and bring the sauce to the boil, stirring all the time. Cook for 2 – 3 minutes, then serve the dish at once.

Piquant Kidneys

SERVES 4

4 tbsp dry sherry
1 tbsp Dijon mustard
dash of Worcestershire sauce
1 tbsp capers, chopped
450 g/1 lb lambs' kidneys, halved and cored
4 tbsp plain flour
½ tsp ground mace
½ tsp dried thyme
salt and freshly ground black pepper
2 tbsp oil
100 g/4 oz rindless bacon rashers, chopped
1 onion, finely chopped
100 g/4 oz button mushrooms, halved
4 tbsp natural yogurt
chopped fresh parsley to serve

Mix the sherry, mustard, Worcestershire sauce and capers and set aside. Toss the kidneys in the flour, mace, thyme and seasoning, ensuring they are evenly coated.

Heat the oil, then stir fry the bacon and onion for about 8 minutes, unitl the bacon is browned and the onion softened. Add the kidneys and stir fry briskly for about 6 minutes, until they are sealed and browned. Tip the mushrooms into the pan and continue stir frying for a further 5 minutes. Lastly add the sherry mixture. Cook, stirring slightly less vigorously, until the juices are bubbling hot and the kidneys are cooked through.

Transfer the kidney mixture to serving plates and top each portion with a little yogurt and plenty of parsley.

PIQUANT KIDNEYS

Paprika Liver

Serve this liver with sweet peppers on a bed of cooked noodles and offer a crisp green salad as an accompaniment.

SERVES 4

350 g/12 oz lambs' liver, cut in strips
4 tbsp plain flour
1 tbsp paprika
salt and freshly ground black pepper
knob of butter
2 tbsp oil
1 garlic clove, crushed

1 onion, thinly sliced
1 red pepper, seeded and thinly sliced
1 green pepper, seeded and thinly sliced
100 ml/4 fl oz chicken stock
15 oz/425 g can chopped tomatoes
12 pimiento-stuffed green olives, sliced

Toss the liver with the flour, paprika and plenty of seasoning. Heat the butter and oil, then stir fry the garlic, onion and peppers for 8 minutes, or until softened. Push this mixture to one side of the pan and stir fry the liver strips fairly briskly, until evenly browned and just cooked.

Pour in the stock and tomatoes and bring to the boil, stirring frequently. Simmer for 5 minutes, stirring occasionally. Taste for seasoning and then add the stuffed olives to the dish.

FLAGEOLET BEANS WITH SPINACH

Flageolet Beans with Spinach

This no-fuss, no-meat main course is ideal for summer days when spare time is best spent outdoors rather than slaving for hours in a hot kitchen.

SERVES 4

450 g/1 lb fresh spinach, trimmed and washed
knob of butter
2 tbsp olive oil
6 spring onions, chopped
2 × 425 g/15 oz cans flageolet beans, drained
2 small courgettes, trimmed and thinly sliced
2 tbsp chopped fresh mint
several large basil sprigs, leaves shredded
225 g/8 oz feta cheese, crumbled
salt and freshly ground black pepper

Press all the spinach leaves into a large saucepan while still dripping wet. Put a lid on the pan and place it over high heat. Cook, shaking the pan often, for about 5 minutes, or until the spinach has wilted and shrunk. Stir the leaves, cover and cook for a further 2 minutes or so, until tender. Drain well, then replace the spinach in the pan and add the knob of butter. Cover and leave over low heat to keep hot.

Heat the oil, then stir fry the spring onions, flageolet beans and courgettes for 5 minutes, until the courgettes are just cooked. Spoon the spinach on to one large or four individual serving plates. Toss the mint, basil and feta into the vegetables, and add seasoning to taste. Spoon the vegetables over the spinach and then serve the dish at once.

Sultan's Liver

SERVES 4

175 g/6 oz roasted buckwheat, cooked (see page 000)
1 small aubergine, trimmed and cut in small cubes
salt and freshly ground black pepper
4 tbsp olive oil
350 g/12 oz lambs' liver, cut in thin strips
2 garlic cloves, crushed
4 cloves
1 cinnamon stick
3 tbsp pine kernels
50 g/2 oz sultanas
2 tsp dried oregano
450 g/1 lb tomatoes, peeled, seeded and quartered

Cook the buckwheat, cover it and set aside ready for serving. Meanwhile, place the aubergine cubes in a colander or sieve and sprinkle them with salt. Place over a basin and leave to drain for 15 minutes, then rinse and pat dry on absorbent kitchen paper.

Heat the oil, then stir fry the liver strips, garlic, cloves and cinnamon stick until just firm – about 3 minutes. Add the aubergine, pine nuts, sultanas, oregano and seasoning, then continue to stir fry until the liver is cooked and the aubergine is just cooked but not soft.

Finally, stir in the tomatoes and continue to cook, stirring, for 5 minutes until all the ingredients are cooked and the flavours well combined.

Fork the buckwheat and place on one large or four individual serving dishes. Divide the liver mixture between them and serve at once.

A MEAL IN A PAN

This chapter includes a broad selection of recipes that are satisfying and balanced enough to form a complete main course. They range from dishes such as Fishballs with Noodles or Minted Lamb with Lentils, which are suitable for informal meals with friends, to Sprouts with Salami or Bread and Bacon Supper, which are ideal mid-week suppers.

Although they are sufficient alone, a fresh side salad always complements a one-pot main dish and some warm bread – whether pitta, nan, white or wholemeal – is an acceptable offering for scooping up the last of the cooking juices.

If you are cooking for more than two, then make sure you have a good sized pan – a skillet or sauté pan if not a wok – to hold all the ingredients. Take the pan to the table or go for informal bowls as serving vessels. If you find them comfortable to use, remember that chopsticks are ideal for eating many mixed dishes as well as Chinese specialities.

GOLDEN FISH WITH POTATOES

Golden Fish with Potatoes

SERVES 4

4 tbsp plain flour
½ tsp turmeric
salt and freshly ground white
    pepper
grated rind of 1 lemon
450 g/1 lb monkfish, thick cod
    fillet or other firm white fish,
    skinned and cubed

3 tbsp oil
2 celery sticks, thinly sliced
1 small onion, finely chopped
225 g/8 oz French beans,
    blanched in boiling water for 1
    minute and drained
675 g/1½ lb small new potatoes,
    scraped and cooked

Mix the flour, turmeric, seasoning and lemon rind, then toss the fish cubes in this mixture to coat them completely.

Heat the oil, then stir fry the celery and onion until slightly softened, about 7 minutes. Add the beans and potatoes and continue to stir fry for 5 – 7 minutes, until all the vegetables are hot and tender.

Push the vegetables to one side of the pan and add the fish. Stir fry the cubes over medium to high heat, taking care not to break them, until golden brown. Gently mix the ingredients and serve at once.

Fishballs with Noodles

SERVES 4

450 g/1 lb white fish, skinned and
    cut in chunks
3 tbsp cornflour
1 egg white
salt and freshly ground white
    pepper
350 g/12 oz Chinese egg noodles
3 tbsp oil
4 thin slices fresh root ginger

1 piece lemon grass or strip of
    lemon rind
1 stick celery, cut diagonally into
    thin slices
1 bunch spring onions, sliced
100 g/4 oz mange-tout peas,
    trimmed
3 tbsp soy sauce
3 tbsp dry sherry

Pound the fish with the cornflour until it is reduced to a paste, then work in the egg white and seasoning. Wet your hands and shape the mixture into small balls, kneading it together so that the fish binds well.

Place the noodles in the pan and pour in enough boiling water to cover them. Bring back to the boil and cook for 2 minutes, then drain the noodles and set aside.

Heat the oil, then stir fry the ginger and lemon grass or lemon rind for 1 minute before adding the fish balls. Stir fry the fish balls until firm and lightly browned. Add the celery, spring onions and mange-tout peas, and continue to stir fry for 5 – 8 minutes, or until the vegetables are slightly tender but not soft.

Add the noodles, soy sauce and sherry, and stir the mixture over high heat until the noodles are hot. Serve the dish at once.

Szechuan Noodles

SERVES 4

350 g/12 oz Chinese egg
  noodles
1 tbsp cornflour
2 tbsp dry sherry
4 tbsp chicken stock
4 tbsp light soy sauce
4 tbsp oil
2 green chillies, seeded and
  chopped
2 garlic cloves, crushed
5 cm/2 in piece fresh root ginger,
  peeled and cut into fine strips

225 g/8 oz lean boneless pork,
  cut into fine strips
1 red pepper, seeded and cut into
  fine, short strips
1 bunch spring onions, cut
  diagonally into fine slices
200 g/7 oz can bamboo shoots,
  drained and cut in strips
2.5 cm/1 in slice Chinese cabbage
  head, separated into pieces

Place the noodles in the pan and pour in enough boiling water to cover them. Bring back to the boil and cook for 2 minutes, then drain the noodles. While the noodles are cooking, blend the cornflour with the sherry, stock and soy sauce, then set aside.

Wipe the pan and heat the oil. Add the noodles, spreading them out thinly, and fry over medium to high heat until they are crisp and golden underneath, patting them down slightly into a thin cake – they will set more or less in shape. Use a large slice to turn the noodles over and brown the second side. Don't worry if the noodles break up slightly – the aim is to end up with some that are crisp and others that remain soft. Transfer the noodles to a large serving dish and keep hot.

Add the chillies, garlic, ginger and pork to the oil remaining in the pan. Stir fry the mixture over high heat until the pork is browned. Add the pepper and spring onions and stir fry for a further 2 minutes before adding the bamboo shoots. Stir fry for 1 minute to heat the bamboo shoots.

Give the cornflour mixture a stir and pour it into the pan. Bring to the boil, stirring, and cook over high heat for 30 seconds. Mix in the Chinese cabbage, stir for less than a minute to heat the cabbage. Spoon the pork mixture over the noodles and serve at once.

Lamb with Chick Peas and Fennel

Lamb and chick peas are natural partners flavourwise, and crunchy, aromatic fennel adds a bit of 'zing' to one of my favourite meals in a pan.

SERVES 4

salt and freshly ground black pepper

350 g/12 oz lean boneless lamb, cut into fine strips (leg steaks or fillet are ideal)

freshly grated nutmeg

1 tsp dried oregano

3 rosemary sprigs

1 garlic clove, crushed (optional)

100 ml/4 fl oz red wine (use a full-bodied one if possible)

3 tbsp olive oil

1 small onion, halved and thinly sliced

2 fennel bulbs, thinly sliced

2 × 425 g/15 oz cans chick peas, drained

2 tsp arrowroot

Season the lamb well, then mix in a good sprinkling of nutmeg, the oregano, rosemary and garlic, if used. Pour in the wine, cover and leave to marinate for a couple of hours or longer if possible (overnight if time allows).

Heat the oil and stir fry the onion for 5 minutes. Use a slotted spoon to add the lamb to the pan, reserving the marinating liquid. Stir fry the meat over fairly high heat until all the strips are browned. Add the fennel and continue stir frying for about 10 minutes, reducing the heat to prevent the meat from overcooking. The fennel should be slightly tender but not softened.

Add the chick peas and stir fry for 2 – 3 minutes to heat them through. Pour in the reserved marinade and bring to the boil, stirring. Simmer for 2 minutes.

Blend the arrowroot with 4 tablespoons water, then add it to the pan and stir over medium heat until the liquid boils to form a thin glaze for the ingredients. Remove the pan from the heat at once, or switch the heat off, as the arrowroot thickening will thin down if it is allowed to simmer. Taste for seasoning and serve with chunks of crusty bread to mop up the juices.

Chicken Balls with Rice Sticks

I first made this when I had been rather over generous in preparing chicken balls for a Japanese meal. The leftovers made a terrific stir fry with ribbon rice sticks, mange-tout, cucumber and a variety of other leftover prepared ingredients.

SERVES 4

3 boneless chicken breasts, skinned and minced	2 tsp sugar
4 tbsp plain flour	225 g/8 oz ribbon rice sticks
3 tbsp sake or dry sherry	3 tbsp groundnut oil
5 tbsp soy sauce (use Japanese sauce if possible)	2 small carrots, cut lengthways into very thin strips
1 small egg	225 g/8 oz mange tout, trimmed
1 bunch spring onions	½ cucumber, peeled, halved crossways and thinly sliced lengthways
salt and pepper	

A food processor is ideal for mincing the raw chicken, otherwise it may be done by hand using a chef's large knife and a chopping action: eventually the chicken will progress from being chopped in fine dice into a fine, minced mixture.

Mix the flour with the chicken, pounding the mixture well. Add 1 tablespoon each of the sake or dry sherry and soy sauce, then mix in the egg. Finely chop the white parts from 2 spring onions, then add them to the mixture with the seasoning. When all the ingredients are thoroughly combined the mixture may seem a little soft, but don't worry – if it is too firm at this stage the cooked balls will be slightly tough in texture. Cover the mixture and chill it on a low shelf in the refrigerator for 30 minutes, or put it in the freezer for about 15 minutes.

Heat the remaining sake and soy sauce with the sugar, stirring, then bring the mixture to the boil and boil hard for 1 minute, set aside. It is best to do this in a saucepan but you can use your stir fry pan, then pour the mixture into a large basin, making sure you scrape it all out of the pan by using a plastic spatula. In a wide pan 1 minute's cooking may be too long as the liquid evaporates more speedily.

Slice the remaining spring onions diagonally. Place the rice sticks in the pan and pour in boiling water to cover them. Bring to the boil and cook for 1 – 2 minutes, until just soft. Drain and rinse under cold water.

Wet your hands and shape the chicken mixture into balls, slightly smaller than walnuts – they do not have to be perfect in shape, but if you keep your hands well wetted with cold water the mixture is easier to shape.

Heat the oil and stir fry the chicken balls over medium to high heat, until they are golden brown all over. At first they should be coaxed and stirred around the pan gently until the mixture firms. If they are stirred smoothly and constantly they will form neat balls. Then they may be stir fried with more vigour so that they brown evenly and cook through. Use a slotted spoon to remove the chicken balls from the pan, adding them to the boiled soy sauce mixture. Toss the balls in the sauce to coat them completely.

Add the carrots, mange-tout and spring onions to the oil remaining in the pan and stir fry the vegetables for about 3 minutes before adding the cucumber. Continue stir frying for about 2 minutes, until the vegetables are just cooked and piping hot. Now, toss in the rice sticks (you may have to rinse them quickly under cold water if they have set in a block – shake off excess water) and stir fry them for a minute or so to heat them up. Replace the chicken balls in the pan and mix well, then serve.

Sprouts with Salami

SERVES 4

2 tbsp tomato purée	2 bay leaves
4 tbsp red wine	salt and freshly ground black pepper
2 tbsp oil	100 g/4 oz salami, cut into fine strips (use good-quality Italian salami for best results)
450 g/1 lb Brussels sprouts, halved	2 × 425 g/15 oz cans borlotti beans, drained
1 small onion, halved and thinly sliced	
1 green pepper, seeded and thinly sliced	

Mix the tomato purée with the wine and 2 – 3 table-spoons of water to make a slightly thickened glaze for adding at the end of stir frying.

Heat the oil, then stir fry the sprouts, onion, pepper and bay leaves with some seasoning over medium heat for 10 minutes, until the sprouts are slightly tender. Add the salami, increase the heat and stir fry for a further 2 minutes before adding the borlotti beans and tomato glaze. Stir for another 2 – 3 minutes or so, until the beans are hot and the mixture is moist with bubbling glaze. Taste for seasoning before serving – open-textured, flat and floury Italian bread is an excellent accompaniment when available.

SPROUTS WITH SALAMI

Mustard Rabbit

This is a good everyday dish, but healthwise it is best to reserve the generous use of butter for frying the bread as an occasional treat.

SERVES 4

1 short French loaf, sliced (see method)
4 tbsp olive oil
50 g/2 oz butter
plenty of chopped fresh parsley
2 tbsp chopped fresh mint (optional)
450 g/1 lb boneless rabbit meat, cut into small cubes
1 tbsp plain flour
4 tbsp mild wholegrain mustard
salt and freshly ground black pepper
3 tbsp oil
900 g/2 lb potatoes, cut in large dice
225 g/8 oz pickling onions
1 carrot, diced
225 g/8 oz shelled peas (blanched fresh or frozen)
250 ml/8 fl oz chicken stock

The French bread slices should not be too thin nor too thick – just under 2.5 cm/1 in. Discard the end pieces. Heat the oil and butter, then quickly toss all the bread slices into the pan and stir fry them until crisp and golden. Do not leave the slices to sit in the oil and butter or they will absorb the fat unevenly, leaving some slices dry. Toss the parsley and mint, if used, into the pan and mix the herbs with the bread. Set the bread aside.

Coat the rabbit cubes with flour, then mix in the mustard and seasoning to coat all the pieces evenly. Heat the oil and stir fry the potatoes for 5 minutes. Add the onions and carrot, then continue stir frying until the potatoes are lightly browned and the onions are just tender. Add the rabbit and continue stir frying until all the pieces are lightly browned.

Stir in the peas and cook for a couple of minutes if they are frozen before pouring in the stock. Bring to the boil, stirring, so that the mustard from the meat thickens the liquid slightly. Cook at a rapid simmer for 2 – 3 minutes, then taste and adjust the seasoning before serving in individual dishes or bowls. Garnish with some of the French bread and offer the rest separately.

● Egg Fried Rice with Prawns

Crunchy water chestnuts add a pleasing contrast in texture to this favourite rice dish.

SERVES 4

225 g/8 oz long-grain rice, cooked
3 tbsp oil
1 tsp sesame oil
1 bunch spring onions, shredded diagonally

200 g/7 oz can water chestnuts, drained and sliced
100 g/4 oz frozen peas
350 g/12 oz peeled cooked prawns
3 eggs, beaten
3 tbsp light soy sauce
whole cooked prawns to garnish

The rice should be freshly cooked. Heat the oils together, then stir fry the onions, water chestnuts and peas for 3 – 5 minutes, until the peas are thawed and hot. Add the prawns and stir fry for another minute.

Lower the heat, pour the eggs into the pan and cook until they are half set. They should be thickened, but not scrambled – if they are too thin, they coat the rice grains too freely and give the finished rice an inferior texture. If the eggs are allowed to set before the rice is added, they tend to be overcooked and slightly rubbery in the finished dish.

Tip all the rice into the pan and turn it over in the egg mixture to combine all the ingredients evenly. The eggs should finish cooking almost immediately if the rice is hot. Sprinkle in the soy sauce and serve at once, garnished with the whole prawns, if liked.

RICE WITH PORK AND PEPPERS

Rice with Pork and Peppers

SERVES 4

3 tbsp oil
1 large onion, thinly sliced
350 g/12 oz lean boneless pork, cut in thin strips
1 red pepper, seeded and thinly sliced
1 green pepper, seeded and thinly sliced

salt and freshly ground black pepper
a little grated nutmeg
grated rind of 1 orange
100 g/4 oz long-grain rice, freshly cooked
100 g/4 oz wild rice, freshly cooked

Heat the oil and stir fry the onion for 2 minutes before adding the pork. Stir fry the meat and onion together until the meat is cooked through and lightly browned, keeping the heat fairly high to seal the strips of meat. Add the peppers, seasoning, nutmeg and orange rind. Reduce the heat slightly and stir fry for 3 – 5 minutes, or until the peppers are cooked.

Stir in both types of rice and cook for a few minutes so that the ingredients are well combined. If the rice has been allowed to cool, it should be reheated thoroughly at this stage – the result is best if the rice is freshly cooked and piping hot when added to the pan.

Five-Spice Pork with Noodles

SERVES 4

450 g/1 lb lean boneless pork, cut in thin slices
½ tsp five-spice powder
salt and freshly ground black pepper
2 spring onions, finely chopped
1 garlic clove, crushed

225 g/8 oz Chinese egg noodles
4 tbsp groundnut oil
225 g/8 oz can bamboo shoots, sliced
225 g/8 oz mange-tout peas, trimmed
3 tbsp soy sauce
2 tbsp roasted sesame seeds

Mix the pork with the five-spice powder, seasoning, spring onions and garlic. Cover and leave to marinate for at least an hour or as long as overnight.

Cover the noodles with boiling water and bring back to the boil. Cook for 2 minutes, then drain and rinse under cold water.

Heat the oil and stir fry the pork until well browned. Add the bamboo shoots and mange-tout, and continue to stir fry for 3 – 4 minutes, or until the vegetables are cooked. Push the meat mixture to one side of the pan or make a space in the middle and add the noodles. Stir the noodles for 2 minutes to heat them through, then stir in the other ingredients, soy sauce and sesame seeds. Cook for 1 minute before serving.

FIVE-SPICE PORK WITH NOODLES

● Lentils with Mushrooms and Almonds

A delicious vegetarian main course, this is an ideal mid-week feast as a change from meat-based main dishes.

SERVES 4

225 g/8 oz green lentils, cooked	4 tbsp olive oil
450 g/1 lb button mushrooms, sliced	75 g/3 oz blanched almonds, split in half
1 tsp ground mace	knob of butter
salt and pepper	225 g/8 oz oyster mushrooms
	4 tbsp snipped chives

The lentils should be freshly cooked, drained and set aside in a covered pan so that they stay hot while the mushrooms are stir fried.

Mix the mushrooms with the mace and plenty of seasoning. Heat the oil and stir fry the mushrooms briskly until they begin to brown. When they give up their juices, continue stir frying until all the liquid has evaporated and the mushrooms are greatly reduced in volume. At this stage they have a good, concentrated flavour; they should be dark in colour and the majority of the liquid in the pan should be the remainder of the oil in which they have cooked.

Use a slotted spoon to remove the mushrooms from the pan and add them to the lentils. Cover and set aside. Stir fry the almonds in the oil remaining in the pan until they are golden, then add them to the lentils. Fork the almonds and mushrooms into the lentils, then transfer the mixture to a serving dish or individual bowls.

Melt the butter in the pan and stir fry the oyster mushrooms over fairly high heat for a minute or so – they should be very lightly cooked. If the mushrooms are overcooked they will collapse. Stir in the chives with a little seasoning and spoon the mixture over the lentils, scraping any juices from the cooking pan. Serve at once.

Minted Lamb with Vegetables

SERVES 4

450 g/1 lb lean boneless lamb, diced
2 tbsp plain flour
salt and freshly ground black pepper
2 tbsp oil
knob of butter
225 g/8 oz small pickling onions

900 g/2 lb small new potatoes, boiled until tender
225 g/8 oz mange-tout
250 ml/8 fl oz dry white wine
4 tbsp chopped fresh mint
1 head endive, roughly shredded, to serve
mint sprigs to garnish

Toss the lamb with the flour and seasoning. Heat the oil and butter, then stir fry the onions for about 10 minutes, until they are lightly browned. Add the meat and stir fry for a further 8 – 10 minutes, until both meat and onions are browned and the onions are tender.

Stir in the potatoes and mange-tout and continue to stir fry for 5 minutes or so, until the potatoes are hot and the mange-tout are lightly cooked. Pour in the wine and bring to the boil. Boil rapidly, stirring, for 2 minutes, so that the ingredients are coated in a lightly thickened glaze. Taste and adjust the seasoning.

Stir in the mint just before turning the lamb mixture out on to a bed of endive, either on one large dish or on individual plates.   Garnish the dish with mint sprigs.

MINTED LAMB WITH VEGETABLES

SESAME CHICK PEAS WITH CHICKEN

Sesame Chick Peas with Chicken

Transform leftover cooked chicken into a tasty meal, in fact this recipe may be used for any cooked meat or poultry.

SERVES 4

1 lettuce heart, shredded
5 cm/2 in piece cucumber, peeled and diced
1 bunch radishes, sliced
2 tbsp roasted sesame seeds
4 tbsp olive oil
2 × 425 g/15 oz cans chick peas, drained
450 g/1 lb cooked chicken, diced

6 tbsp tahini
4 tbsp snipped chives
2 tbsp chopped fresh parsley
salt and freshly ground black pepper
2 avocados, halved, stoned, peeled and cut in chunks
50 g/2 oz stoned black olives, halved
1 lemon, cut into wedges

Mix the lettuce, cucumber, radishes and sesame seeds, then arrange this salad around the edge of four serving plates or one large dish.

Heat the oil, then stir fry the chick peas and chicken for about 5 minutes, or until the chicken is thoroughly heated. Stir in the tahini until it combines with the oil to coat the ingredients in a creamy dressing. Add the herbs, seasoning and avocados, then stir the black olives into the mixture.

Divide the chicken mixture between the serving plates and garnish with lemon wedges. The lemon juice should be squeezed over the chicken mixture and salad.

● Pork-Filled Taco Shells

SERVES 4

2 tbsp oil
1 onion, chopped
1 green pepper, seeded and diced
2 celery sticks, thinly sliced
225 g/8 oz minced pork
salt
¼ tsp cayenne pepper
425 g/15 oz can red kidney beans, drained
425 g/15 oz can chopped tomatoes
Tabasco sauce to taste
2 avocados, halved, stoned and diced
grated rind and juice of 1 lime
8 taco shells
shredded lettuce to serve

Heat the oil, then stir fry the onion, pepper and celery until softened before adding the pork to the pan. Sprinkle in salt and the cayenne pepper, then stir fry the meat until it is cooked and well-browned.

Add the kidney beans and tomatoes, then stir fry for a further 5 minutes. Lastly, add Tabasco sauce to taste and remove the pan from the heat.

Toss the avocados with the lime rind and juice. Spoon some of the meat mixture into each taco shell and top with avocado. Arrange the filled shells supported on a bed of shredded lettuce and serve at once.

● Bacon with Aubergines and Walnuts

SERVES 4

2 large aubergines, trimmed and cubed
salt and freshly ground black pepper
6 tbsp olive oil
3 leeks, thinly sliced
225 g/8 oz rindless bacon rashers, roughly chopped
75 g/3 oz walnut pieces
225 g/8 oz small mushrooms, halved
plenty of chopped fresh parsley or shredded basil leaves

Place the aubergines in a colander, sprinkle them with salt and set aside over a bowl for 15 minutes. Rinse well and pat dry on absorbent kitchen paper.

Heat the oil and stir fry the leeks for 5 minutes until softened. Add the aubergine pieces and continue stir frying until they are lightly browned on the outside, and tender but not soft. Stir in the bacon and walnuts, then continue cooking until the bacon is cooked and the aubergines are softened.

Add the mushrooms with seasoning and stir fry for a further 3 minutes, to heat the mushrooms through without overcooking them. Taste for seasoning before serving sprinkled with parsley or basil. Wholemeal rolls or pitta bread are ideal accompaniments.

Tofu Chow Mein

SERVES 4

4 large dried Chinese mushrooms
4 tbsp soy sauce
2 tbsp dry sherry
1 garlic clove, crushed
¼ tsp five spice powder
225 g/8 oz tofu, cubed
2 tsp cornflour
225 g/8 oz Chinese egg noodles

3 tbsp groundnut oil
1 small carrot, cut into matchstick strips
1 yellow pepper, cut into short thin strips
6 spring onions, sliced diagonally
200 g/7 oz can water chestnuts, drained and sliced
225 g/8 oz beansprouts

Place the dried mushrooms in a small basin or mug and pour in just enough hot water to cover them. Use a saucer or base of a second mug to press the mushrooms down and keep them submerged. Leave to soak for 20 minutes.

Mix the soy sauce, sherry, garlic and five spice powder, then pour this mixture over the tofu and set aside.

Drain the mushrooms, reserving the liquid. Discard their tough stalks, then slice the caps. Blend the cornflour to a paste with the soaking liquid.

Place the noodles in the pan and pour in boiling water to cover them. Bring to the boil and cook for 2 minutes, then drain and spread out on a heated serving dish. Cover with foil and keep hot.

Heat the oil. Drain any liquid from the tofu into the cornflour liquid, then stir fry the tofu over high heat until golden all over. Take care at first not to break the pieces – once the tofu is crisp outside it is less likely to break up.

Add the carrot, pepper, mushrooms and spring onions and stir fry until the vegetables are slightly softened. Add the water chestnuts and continue to stir fry for 2 minutes, or until hot.

Give the cornflour liquid a stir and pour it into the pan. Bring to the boil, stirring, and simmer for 1 minute. Add the beansprouts and cook, stirring for 1 minute, to heat them. Pour the mixture over the noodles and serve the dish at once.

Curried Pork with Beans

The quality of the curry powder determines the flavour of the finished dish – buy a reputable brand or mix your own spices.

SERVES 4

450 g/1 lb lean boneless pork, diced
3 tbsp oil or ghee
1 large onion, thinly sliced
2 × 426 g/15 oz cans red kidney beans, drained
3 tbsp chopped coriander leaves

MARINADE

salt and freshly ground black pepper
1 tbsp curry powder
2.5 cm/1 in piece fresh root ginger, finely grated
1 onion, grated
2 garlic cloves, crushed
1 tbsp tomato purée
juice of 1 lemon
100 ml/4 fl oz natural yogurt

Place the meat in a dish and add all the marinade ingredients. Mix well, then cover and leave the pork to marinate overnight.

Drain the meat well, reserving the marinade. Heat the oil or ghee, then stir fry the onion for about 15 minutes, or until lightly browned. Add the meat and continue stir frying until all the pieces are cooked. Stir in the kidney beans and pour in any reserved marinade, then continue to cook, stirring, for 15 minutes. Serve at once, sprinkled with fresh coriander.

CURRIED PORK WITH BEANS

◗ Vegetable Pancakes

If you do not want to make pancakes, the stir fried vegetables may be served in pitta bread, as a topping for baked potatoes or in a split baguette. They can, of course, be served quite simply by themselves with a couple of slices of wholemeal bread to fill hungry diners!

SERVES 4

2 carrots, cut in matchstick strips
2 leeks, cut into short thin strips
½ celeriac, cut in matchstick strips
1 red or yellow pepper, seeded and cut into short thin strips
250 ml/8 oz medium cider
100 g/4 oz ready-to-eat dried apricots, sliced
2 large tarragon sprigs, leaves removed
1 bay leaf

2 tbsp olive oil
50 g/2 oz slivered almonds
2 courgettes, cut into short thin strips
175 g/6 oz soft cheese with garlic and herbs

PANCAKES

75 g/3 oz wholemeal flour
salt and pepper
2 eggs
300 ml/½ pint milk
1 tbsp oil plus oil for cooking

Combine the carrots, leeks, celeriac and pepper with the cider, apricots, tarragon leaves and bay leaf in a dish. Cover and set aside to marinate.

Next make the pancakes: turn the flour into a bowl and mix in a little seasoning. Make a well in the middle, then add the eggs and some of the milk. Gradually beat the eggs and milk into the flour to make a smooth batter, adding more milk as the mixture thickens. Beat well until smooth. If possible set aside for 20 minutes before cooking. Stir in 1 tablespoon oil before frying the batter to make eight large thin pancakes. If the batter thickens on standing, add a little water.

Layer the cooked pancakes with pieces of absorbent kitchen paper to prevent them sticking together, and cover the stack with foil. Keep them hot.

Drain the vegetables and apricots, reserving the liquid. Heat the olive oil and stir fry the almonds until lightly browned. Add the drained vegetables and apricots, and stir fry until the leek and celeriac are just tender. Add the courgettes and stir fry for 3 – 5 minutes before pouring in the reserved cider marinade with seasoning to taste.

Bring the cooking liquid to the boil, then stir in the soft cheese and remove the pan from the heat. Use a draining spoon to place some vegetables on a pancake, then fold it into four and place it on a serving dish or individual plate. Arrange any leftover vegetables on the serving dish with the pancakes, spooning extra into the pancake cones. Pour the sauce around the pancakes and serve at once.

Bread and Bacon Supper

This is unusual, interesting and delicious.

SERVES 4

½ head endive, trimmed and broken into pieces
1 small red onion, thinly sliced and separated into rings
4 tomatoes, peeled, seeded and cut in thin wedges
6 tbsp olive oil
1 garlic clove, crushed
1 short French loaf, cut into chunks (or use any other crusty bread)

225 g/8 oz rindless bacon rashers, roughly chopped
225 g/8 oz button mushrooms
salt and freshly ground black pepper
plenty of chopped fresh parsley
1 lemon, cut into wedges

Make a salad from the endive, onion and tomatoes, then divide it between serving plates or dishes.

Heat the oil and garlic, then stir fry the chunks of bread until they are just beginning to brown. Add the bacon to the pan and continue stir frying until the bread is part-browned and slightly crisp. The bacon should be cooked. Toss in the mushrooms, seasoning and the parsley, and stir for 2 minutes to cook the mushrooms very lightly. Divide the bread and bacon mixture between the prepared salads and add the lemon wedges for their juice.

Wheaten Aubergines

This is a hot dish inspired by the classic wheat salad known as tabbouleh.

SERVES 4

2 large aubergines, cut into cubes
salt and freshly ground black pepper
225 g/8 oz bulgur
about 6 tsp olive oil
1 garlic clove

1 tsp dried marjoram
4 tbsp pine kernels
4 tbsp raisins
1 bunch spring onions, chopped
4 tbsp chopped fresh mint
1 lemon, cut into wedges
mint sprigs to garnish

Place the aubergines in a colander and sprinkle with salt, then place over a bowl to drain for 20 minutes. Place the bulgur in a basin and pour in enough cold water to cover it. Set aside to soak for 15 minutes.

Rinse and thoroughly drain the aubergines. Heat some olive oil and add the garlic, then stir fry the aubergines, adding more oil as needed, until they are lightly browned and tender. Add the marjoram, pine kernels and raisins, and continue stir frying the mixture for a minute or so.

Drain the bulgur and tip it into the pan, then stir it with the aubergines for a few minutes, until it is hot. Mix in the spring onions and mint, and serve. Add the lemon wedges so that their juice may be squeezed over the aubergine mixture. Garnish with mint sprigs.

Saffron Prawns with Nan

SERVES 4

2 tsp saffron strands
1 garlic clove, crushed
5 cm/2 in piece fresh root ginger, finely chopped
6 green cardamoms, slightly crushed
2 bay leaves
1 cinnamon stick, broken
4 tbsp coriander seeds, lightly crushed

1 tbsp cumin seeds
salt and freshly ground black pepper
450 g/1 lb peeled cooked prawns
4 nan bread
50 g/2 oz butter
1 large onion, finely chopped
100 g/4 oz frozen peas
4 tbsp chopped fresh coriander
1 lemon, cut into wedges
coriander sprigs to garnish

Pound the saffron strands to a powder, then stir in 2 tablespoons boiling water. Mix in the garlic, ginger, cardamoms, bay leaves, cinnamon, coriander, cumin and seasoning. Pour this mixture over the prawns, scraping every last drop of saffron liquid from the container. Mix the spices with the prawns, cover and leave to marinate for 1 hour – or longer if necessary if time permits.

Heat the nan under the grill on a medium setting. Melt the butter and stir fry the onion for 5 minutes. Then add the prawns and peas and stir fry for a further 5 – 7 minutes, until the spices and peas are cooked. Taste for seasoning, then pile the prawn mixture to one side of each piece of nan. Sprinkle with coriander and add a lemon wedge next to the prawns. Garnish with coriander. Squeeze the lemon juice over the prawns just before they are eaten.

SAFFRON PRAWNS, SERVED HERE WITH PITTA

● Couscous with Ham and Cabbage

This is an unusual way of presenting couscous, but it is quite successful.

SERVES 4

225 g/8 oz couscous
3 tbsp olive oil
1 large onion, halved and thinly sliced
450 g/1 lb pumpkin flesh, cut in small cubes
2 thyme sprigs
½ small green cabbage, finely shredded

350 g/12 oz cooked ham, shredded
4 large tomatoes, peeled and cut into eighths
salt and freshly ground black pepper
50 g/2 oz butter, melted
plenty of chopped fresh parsley

Place the couscous in a heatproof dish. Pour on freshly boiling water to cover it by 2.5 cm/1 in, cover and set aside for 15 minutes, by which time the grains will have swollen and they will be ready to serve.

Heat the oil, then stir fry the onion, pumpkin and thyme together for 6 – 8 minutes, or until the pumpkin is just tender.

Add the cabbage and continue stir frying to lightly cook the cabbage. Toss in the ham and tomatoes and cook briefly to heat both ingredients. Taste and add seasoning to taste.

Pour the melted butter over the couscous and fork up the grains. Turn the couscous into a large dish or into individual bowls and pile the cabbage mixture in the middle. Sprinkle with parsley and serve at once.

STIRRING UP SOMETHING SPECIAL

Just to prove that stir frying can produce smart results, this chapter has plenty of ideas to grace any formal dinner party menu.

When planning a formal menu, balance a main dish that is cooked at the last minute by having accompaniments that are ready in advance. For example, have gratin-style vegetables, rice and pasta that can be cooked or popped in the oven just before the meal commences, so that you can focus all your attention on the stir frying rather than trying to drain or steam vegetables or fiddle with exacting side dishes. If you are cooking pasta as an accompaniment, use the fresh type that cooks in a couple of minutes or cook the dried type before serving the main course and transfer it to a serving dish. If it is very slightly undercooked and tossed in oil or butter with seasoning it will outlast the majority of starters, covered and kept in a warm oven.

Remember that the finishing touches are all important to the appearance of the finished dish, so think about garnishes in advance and have them prepared, covered and kept cool if necessary. Lastly, when you clear the appetizer and exit from the dining area, let your guests know that you are about to create a splendid last-minute dish and warn them that they have a few minutes to wait.

Salmon Indienne

Salmon steaks may be used instead of fillet – cut out the bone, then cut the fish into chunks. For a less expensive alternative, look for tail pieces. Wild rice mixed with a little chopped fresh coriander is a good accompaniment to this dish. It adds both texture and flavour to complement the salmon.

SERVES 4

900 g/2 lb salmon fillet
10 green cardamoms
1 tbsp ground coriander
grated rind and juice of 1 lime
1 garlic clove, crushed
2.5 cm/1 in piece fresh root ginger, peeled and chopped
1 green chilli, seeded and chopped
2 spring onions, chopped
salt and freshly ground black pepper
2 bay leaves
2 tbsp oil
450 g/1 lb ripe tomatoes, peeled, seeded and roughly chopped (see page 000)
lime wedges to garnish

Trim any skin and bones from the salmon. Cut the salmon into chunks and place in a basin. Split the cardamom pods and place the small black seeds in a pestle. Crush them to a powder with a mortar, then mix in the coriander, lime rind and juice, garlic, ginger, chilli and spring onions. Add plenty of seasoning, then pour the spice mixture over the salmon and mix lightly to coat all the chunks without breaking them up. Tuck the bay leaves in among the chunks. Cover and leave to marinate for about 2 hours or longer, depending on the time available.

Heat the oil, then add the salmon with all the marinating juices and stir fry, taking care not to break the chunks, until the fish it just cooked. Stir in the tomatoes and heat through for 1 minute.

Arrange the fish on a serving platter, picking out the bay leaves as a garnish, and add the wedges of lime. The juice from the lime may be squeezed over the salmon just before it is eaten.

SALMON INDIENNE

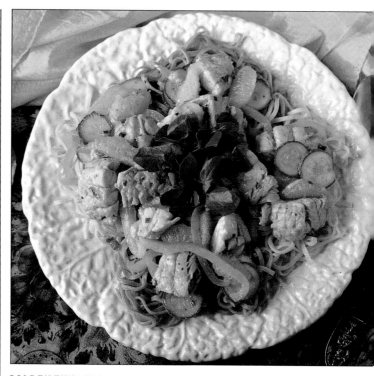

GOLDEN TUNA WITH WATERCRESS

Golden Tuna with Watercress

Swordfish may also be cooked this way instead of the tuna. Serve the cooked mixture in small nests of cooked *paglia e fieno pasta* (thin green and white noodles, straw and hay – look for them in the fresh pasta refrigerator in the supermarket), adding a garnish of small watercress sprigs and halved orange slices.

SERVES 4

4 oranges
450 g/1 lb tuna steak, cubed
6 tbsp olive oil
6 tbsp dry white wine
4 tbsp snipped chives
salt and freshly ground black pepper
1 yellow pepper, seeded and cut into fine strips
4 yellow courgettes, thinly sliced
2 bunches watercress, trimmed

Grate the rind and squeeze the juice from 1 orange, then pour this over the tuna fish. Add all but 1 tablespoon of the olive oil, the wine, chives and seasoning. Mix the fish with the flavouring ingredients and cover. Leave to marinate for 4 – 6 hours before cooking.

Peel the remaining oranges, removing all the pith. Hold each orange in turn over a basin and cut between the membranes to remove the fruit segments. Catch all the juices and pour them over the fish.

Heat the remaining 1 tablespoon olive oil. Drain the tuna and reserve the marinade. Stir fry the fish until lightly browned, then use a slotted spoon to remove it from the pan and set aside. Stir fry the pepper and courgettes for 1 minute, then tip in all the marinade and bring to the boil. Boil rapidly for a minute or so, then replace the tuna and stir in the watercress leaves. Boil for another 30 – 60 seconds and remove from the heat. Carefully mix in the orange and serve at once.

Sizzling Butterfly Prawns

Uncooked Mediterranean or jumbo prawns are available frozen from good fishmongers and oriental supermarkets. Since they tend to be rather expensive, I have kept the portions small but the end result need not look mean with the right accompaniments: for example, serve a chow mein with some sliced scallops.

SERVES 4

24 uncooked Mediterranean prawns, shelled with tails on
cornflour for coating
5 cm/2 in piece fresh root ginger, peeled and grated, then chopped into small pieces
1 garlic clove, crushed
1 green chilli, seeded and finely chopped (optional)
2 tsp sugar
2 tsp white wine vinegar
½ tsp tomato purée
1 tbsp light soy sauce
1 tbsp dry sherry
pinch of five spice powder
1 tsp sesame oil
6 tbsp groundnut oil

VEGETABLE GARNISH

6 spring onions, cut into very fine strips
½ red pepper, seeded and cut into short, very fine strips
¼ cucumber, peeled and cut into short, fine strips
lemon wedges to serve

To prepare the prawns, first remove the fine black cord that runs down the back (this may have been removed). Using a small sharp knife, take a prawn and cut it down the back, almost through in half, then press it open. Repeat with all the shellfish. Coat them generously with cornflour and shake off excess.

In a bowl, mix the ginger, garlic, chilli, sugar, vinegar, tomato purée, soy sauce, sherry, five spice powder and sesame oil. Add the prawns and mix well to coat them with the flavouring ingredients. They should be thoroughly tossed to ensure that they are all flavoured with the paste.

Heat the groundnut oil until it is shimmering hot, then stir fry the prawns over high heat until they are crisp and golden – this takes only a few minutes. Use a slotted spoon to transfer them to a serving plate.

Add all the vegetables for garnish to the oil remaining in the pan and stir fry for 2 minutes. Spoon them on the plate with the prawns and add the lemon wedges. Serve the dish immediately.

Swordfish with Saffron

Any firm white fish is good cooked like this – halibut, monkfish or cod. New potatoes and spinach or a salad are suitable accompaniments.

SERVES 4

675 g/1½ lb swordfish steak, cut in chunks
4 tbsp sunflower oil plus extra for cooking
2 tbsp lemon juice
250 ml/8 fl oz dry white wine
1 bay leaf
1 thyme sprig

salt and freshly ground black pepper
1 tsp saffron strands
4 tbsp plain flour
2 leeks, thinly sliced
2 carrots, cut into matchstick strips
2 celery sticks, thinly sliced
250 ml/8 fl oz single cream

Place the fish in a dish. In a jar with a tight-fitting lid, combine half the oil, the lemon juice, wine, bay leaf, thyme and seasoning. Shake the mixture until the oil is thoroughly combined, then pour it over the fish. Cover and leave to marinate for several hours.

Pound the saffron strands to a powder, then stir in 2 tablespoons boiling water. Stir until the saffron has dissolved completely and set aside.

Drain the fish, reserving the marinade, then mop the cubes on absorbent kitchen paper. Toss them in the flour, adding a little seasoning. Heat the remaining oil and stir fry the fish until golden brown. Use a slotted spoon to transfer the fish to a serving dish or individual plates and keep hot. Add a little extra oil and stir fry the leeks, carrots and celery over high heat for 2 – 3 minutes, until they are lightly cooked.

Arrange the vegetables alongside the fish, then pour the reserved marinade into the pan and bring to the boil. Boil hard until reduced by half, then reduce the heat and stir in the cream. Add the saffron liquid and heat gently to warm the cream. Do not boil. Spoon the sauce over or around the fish and serve at once.

Scallops with Courgettes

This makes a perfect light lunch – serve the seafood mixture on a base of cooked narrow noodles, wild rice or salad.

SERVES 4

2 tbsp olive oil
2 tbsp finely chopped onion
16 scallops, sliced

6 small courgettes, thinly sliced
salt and pepper
4 tarragon sprigs, leaves removed
4 tbsp single cream

Heat the oil and stir fry the onion over moderate heat for about 5 minutes, until softened. Stir fry the scallops for 2 minutes. Add the courgettes, seasoning and tarragon, and cook for a further 2 minutes. Neither the scallops nor the courgettes should be overcooked – the scallops, in particular, will toughen.

Add the cream, stir for a few seconds to heat it through without boiling, then serve at once.

COOK'S TIP

Crisp croûtons go well with the scallops and courgettes. Make them by frying small triangles of bread in a mixture of olive oil and butter until golden. Drain on absorbent kitchen paper, and arrange the croûtons around the edge of the scallop mixture on the dish.

SWORDFISH WITH SAFFRON

DUCK WITH PLUMS AND PORT

Duck with Plums and Port

Serve this rich stir fry with rice or pasta.

SERVES 4

3 duck breasts, skinned and thinly
   sliced across (into medallions)
100 ml/4 fl oz port
grated rind and juice of 1 orange
1 bay leaf
1 parsley sprig
1 thyme sprig
1 rosemary sprig
3 tbsp plain flour

salt and freshly ground black
   pepper
2 tbsp oil
knob of butter
225 g/8 oz plums, halved, stoned
   and quartered

GARNISH (OPTIONAL)
orange slices
fresh herbs

Place the duck in a dish. Add the port, orange rind and juice, and all the herbs. Mix well, cover and leave to marinate overnight.

Strain the duck well, reserving the marinade. Pick out the herbs, then pat the duck on absorbent kitchen paper. Toss the slices of duck in the flour, adding plenty of seasoning.

Heat the oil and butter with the herbs. Add the duck and stir fry the pieces until lightly browned. Sprinkle any leftover flour into the pan, then stir in the marinade and add the plums. Stir all the time until the juices boil and thicken. Reduce the heat and cook for 2 minutes, then taste for seasoning before serving. Halved orange slices and fresh herbs may be added for garnish.

Flambé Chicken with Peaches

Dried peaches give this dish a wonderfully rich, fruity flavour. Rice, pasta and plain, boiled new potatoes are all suitable accompaniments; however, for a lighter meal, the cooked chicken may be served on a crisp salad of mixed leaves, with warm fresh bread.

SERVES 4

100 g/4 oz dried peaches
1 tbsp oil
knob of butter
2 rosemary sprigs
strip of lemon rind
4 boneless chicken breasts,
   skinned and cubed

salt and freshly ground black
   pepper
4 tbsp brandy

GARNISH
1 fresh peach, stoned and sliced
rosemary sprigs

Place the peaches in a small basin, then pour in just enough cold water to cover them. Cover and leave to soak overnight.

Drain the peaches, reserving the liquid, then cut them into small pieces. Heat the oil and butter, then add the rosemary and lemon rind. Stir fry these aromatics for about 30 seconds before adding the chicken – this gives the cooking fat a good flavour. Sprinkle in seasoning, then stir fry the chicken until cooked through.

Pour in the peaches and their soaking liquid, bring to the boil and stir over medium to high heat until most of the liquid has evaporated and the chicken is well glazed and juicy. Transfer the chicken to a serving dish, discarding the lemon rind and cooked rosemary. Garnish the chicken with the fresh peach slices and the sprigs of rosemary.

Add the brandy to the pan (it will still be hot enough to warm the brandy without requiring any further heating) and swirl it around before pouring over the chicken and igniting it. Take the flaming chicken to the table and serve it as soon as the flames have subsided.

COOK'S TIP

To prevent cut peaches from turning brown, dip the pieces in lemon juice and keep them covered until they are used.

Glazed Lamb

The fillet of lamb is the eye of meat cut from the best end or middle neck. Sliced into neat rounds, as here, the portions are referred to as medallions. A border of piped mashed potatoes or small new potatoes will complement the rich, honey glaze which coats the stir fried lamb with plums.

SERVES 4

900 g/2 lb lamb fillet, sliced into neat circles
4 rosemary sprigs
2 tbsp clear honey
250 ml/8 fl oz medium cider
3 tbsp plain flour
salt and freshly ground black pepper
2 tbsp groundnut oil
1 small onion, finely chopped
225 g/8 oz red plums, halved and stoned
rosemary sprigs to garnish

Place the meat in a dish and add the rosemary, honey and cider. Mix well, cover and leave to marinate for several hours or overnight.

Drain the meat well, reserving all the marinade. Then sprinkle the flour and plenty of seasoning over the pieces of lamb.

Heat the oil and stir fry the onion for 3 – 4 minutes. Add the lamb and stir fry until browned all over. Pour in the marinade and add the plums. Boil quite hard for about 2 minutes, so that the marinade reduces and the plums cook. Stir to prevent the meat sticking to the pan. When the meat and plums are well glazed in sauce, transfer them to a serving dish. Add some rosemary sprigs as a garnish.

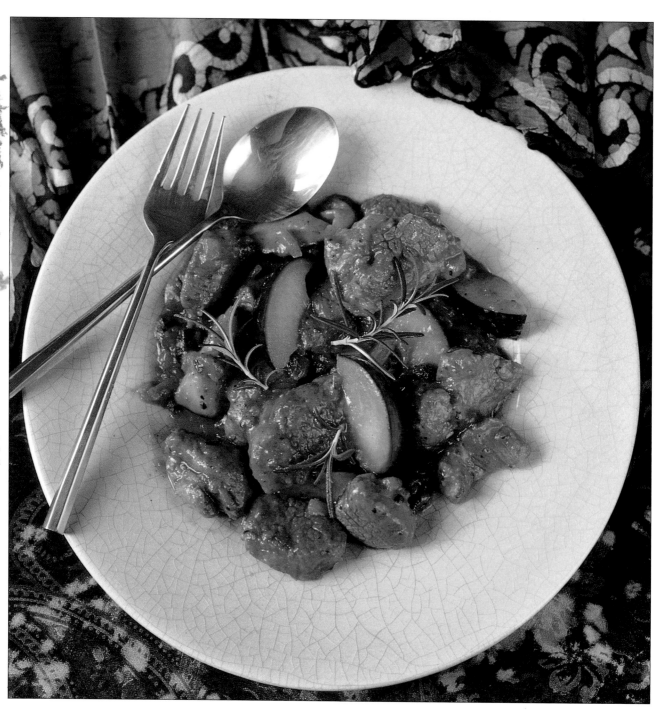

Minted Lamb with Lentils

SERVES 4

225 g/8 oz green lentils
450 g/1 lb lean boneless lamb, diced
1 garlic clove (optional)
2 tbsp chopped fresh mint
salt and freshly ground pepper
2 tbsp olive oil
1 onion, chopped
225 g/8 oz mushrooms, sliced
dash of Worcestershire sauce
450 g/1 lb tomatoes, peeled and roughly chopped
250 ml/8 fl oz Greek-style yogurt
mint sprigs to garnish (optional)

Cook the lentils in plenty of boiling water for 35 minutes or until tender, but not mushy. Drain well and set aside.

Thoroughly mix the lamb with the garlic (if used), mint and plenty of seasoning. Heat the oil and stir fry the onion for 5 minutes before adding the lamb. Continue stir frying until the meat is cooked and well-browned. Stir in the mushrooms and Worcestershire sauce and stir fry for a further 5 minutes.

Tip the lentils into the lamb mixture and stir in the tomatoes. Stir fry for another 3 – 5 minutes so that the lentils and tomatoes are hot. Taste for seasoning, then divide between individual serving dishes and top each portion with a little yogurt. Garnish with mint sprigs, if liked, and serve the remaining yogurt separately.

Oriental Ginger Lamb

A small, local, undistinguished Chinese restaurant includes a number of special dishes on its menu and this is based on one of them – it's very simple, absolutely bursting with flavour and ideal for fellow ginger fans! It is a dish to make when you can buy juicy, young ginger, which is plump and thin skinned – look out for it in Chinese supermarkets. Remember to warn unsuspecting guests that there are whole ginger slices in among the pieces of meat – when the ginger is young and tender, the slices are, of course, perfectly edible, but many people prefer to avoid them.

SERVES 4

450 g/1 lb lean boneless lamb, cut into small, thin slices
5 cm/2 in piece, young fresh root ginger, peeled and very thinly sliced
4 tbsp soy sauce
4 tbsp dry sherry
1 tsp sugar
1 tbsp lemon juice
1 tbsp cornflour
250 ml/8 fl oz lamb or chicken stock
3 tbsp oil
1 tsp sesame oil
1 garlic clove
1 bunch spring onions, cut in 2.5 cm/1 in lengths

Place the lamb in a dish and mix in the ginger. Stir the soy sauce, sherry, sugar and lemon juice together, then pour the mixture over the lamb and ginger. Cover and leave to marinate for several hours.

Blend the cornflour to a smooth paste with a little of the stock, then stir in the remaining stock. Heat the oil and sesame oil, add the garlic and use a slotted spoon to add the lamb and ginger to the pan. Stir fry the lamb until browned, then add the spring onions and continue stir frying for 2 minutes.

Pour in the marinating juices from the lamb and the stock. Bring to the boil and simmer, stirring, for 5 minutes. Taste for seasoning before serving, adding a little extra soy sauce if necessary.

ORIENTAL GINGER LAMB

BEEF IN OYSTER SAUCE

Beef in Oyster Sauce

Include this as part of a Chinese menu, in which case the quantities may be reduced by half, or serve it with plain cooked rice or chow mein.

SERVES 4

450 g/1 lb frying steak, cut into small, thin slices
3 tbsp oyster sauce
2 tbsp soy sauce
1 garlic clove, crushed
4 tbsp dry sherry

4 large dried Chinese mushrooms
4 tbsp oil
1 green pepper, seeded and cut into chunks
1 red pepper, seeded and cut into chunks
1 onion, cut into chunks

Place the meat in a dish. Mix the oyster sauce, soy sauce, garlic and sherry together, then pour the mixture over the meat and mix well. Cover and leave to marinate for 2 – 4 hours. Place the mushrooms in a small basin or mug and pour in just enough hot water to cover them. Place a saucer or the base of another mug on the mushrooms to keep them submerged, then leave to soak for 20 minutes. Drain, reserving the soaking liquid, discard tough stalks and slice the mushroom caps.

Heat the oil, then stir fry the peppers and onion for 3 minutes. Use a draining spoon to add the beef to the pan, then continue stir frying until the meat is cooked and lightly browned. Add the mushrooms.

Pour the soaking liquid into the oyster sauce marinade left from the meat and mix well, then pour the liquid into the pan. Bring to the boil and boil rapidly for a few minutes so that the meat is coated in a slightly thickened sauce. Serve at once.

Beef Stroganoff

This classic dish of quick fried steak with soured cream takes its name from the Russian Count Stroganoff. The colds of northern Siberia rendered the Count's beef virtually frozen, such that it could only be cut into the thinnest slices. Plain cooked rice and a good, very crisp, fresh mixed green salad will make the meal a real treat.

SERVES 4

900 g/2 lb good beef steak (at least rump or topside, fillet if you are feeling extravagent)
salt and freshly ground black pepper
½ tsp paprika
2 tbsp olive oil

large knob of butter
1 onion, halved and thinly sliced
225 g/8 oz mushrooms, thinly sliced
4 tbsp brandy
300 ml/½ pint soured cream
plenty of chopped fresh parsley

Place the meat in the freezer until it is icy and very firm. Use a sharp knife to cut the beef across the grain into the thinnest slices possible, then cut them across into strips. Season the beef and sprinkle with paprika.

Heat the oil and butter, then stir fry the onion for 5 minutes. Add the mushrooms and stir fry for a further 3 minutes, taking care not to break up the mushroom slices. Push the onion and mushrooms to one side of the pan, then stir fry the meat over high heat until all the strips are browned.

Sprinkle in the brandy and mix the meat with the onion and mushrooms. Pour in the cream and heat briefly without allowing it to boil. Quickly toss in plenty of parsley and serve at once.

BEEF STROGANOFF

Marinated Venison with Red Cabbage

Small baked potatoes in their skins or cooked buckwheat (see Pork with Orange), mixed with plenty of chopped parsley, go well with this venison dish.

SERVES 4

450 g/1 lb venison steak (suitable for frying), trimmed of all fat and cut in strips	3 tbsp plain flour
	4 tbsp olive oil
250 ml/8 fl oz red wine	1 large onion, halved and thinly sliced
1 blade of mace	450 g/1 lb red cabbage, finely shredded
1 bay leaf	3 tbsp soft brown sugar
6 juniper berries, crushed	2 tbsp cider vinegar
salt and freshly ground black pepper	

Place the venison in a dish, then add the wine, mace, bay leaf, juniper and plenty of seasoning. Mix well, cover and marinate for 24 hours.

Drain the meat, reserving the marinade. Pat the meat dry on absorbent kitchen paper, then toss it with the flour until it is well mixed.

Heat half the oil and stir fry the onion for 5 minutes. Add the venison and stir fry for about 10 minutes, or until the strips are well browned. Use a slotted spoon to remove the meat from the pan.

Add the remaining oil and stir fry the cabbage for 5 – 7 minutes, or until it is slightly softened. Sprinkle in the sugar and vinegar and add a little seasoning, then stir fry for a further 2 minutes. Replace the meat and mix well, then pour in the reserved marinade. Bring to the boil and simmer for 5 minutes. Discard the blade of mace before serving the venison.

Steak with Anchovies and Olives

Pasta or a classic, creamy risotto are ideal accompaniments for this Italian-style steak stir fry.

SERVES 4

675 g/1½ lb frying steak, cut into strips	1 onion, halved and thinly sliced
	1 green pepper, halved, seeded and thinly sliced
1 garlic clove, crushed	50 g/2 oz can anchovy fillets, drained and chopped
2 tbsp tomato purée	
250 ml/8 fl oz red wine	100 g/4 oz black olives, stoned and sliced
salt and freshly ground black pepper	
	2 tbsp chopped parsley
4 tbsp plain flour	handful of basil leaves, coarsely shredded
4 tbsp olive oil	

Place the steak in a dish. Mix the garlic, tomato purée and red wine with seasoning, then pour the mixture over the steak. Mix well, cover and leave the meat to marinate overnight.

Drain the steak, reserving the marinade. Pat the strips of meat dry on absorbent kitchen paper, then toss them in the flour.

STEAK WITH ANCHOVIES AND OLIVES

Heat 3 tablespoons of the olive oil, then stir fry the onion and pepper for 5 minutes. Add the steak and stir fry over fairly high heat until the strips are evenly browned. Pour in the reserved marinade and stir until the sauce boils. Simmer for 5 minutes, stirring, then taste for seasoning before transferring the meat mixture to a serving dish.

Wipe out the pan and heat the remaining olive oil. Add the anchovies, olives and parsley and toss them in the hot oil for 30 seconds. Stir in the basil, then pour the mixture over the steak and serve at once.

DESALTING ANCHOVIES

For a milder less salty result, the anchovy fillets may be drained, soaked in a little milk for 5 minutes, then drained again.

● Pork with Pernod

If you do not have any Pernod, then substitute Greek ouzo or Turkish raki. Rice or couscous will match the full flavour of this simple dish.

SERVES 4

675 g/1½ lb lean boneless pork, diced
2 sage sprigs
2 thyme sprigs
100 ml/4 fl oz Pernod or other aniseed liquor
salt and freshly ground black pepper
2 tbsp olive oil

1 leek, thinly sliced
2 small carrots, diced
225 g/8 oz button mushrooms, sliced
250 ml/8 fl oz soured cream
8 large Iceberg lettuce leaves
tarragon sprigs to garnish (optional)

Place the pork in a dish with the sage and thyme, then pour in the Pernod or other liquor. Add some seasoning, mix well and cover. Leave to marinate for about 2 hours.

Heat the oil, then stir fry the leek and carrots for 5 minutes. Use a draining spoon to add the pork to the pan, with the herb sprigs. Reserve the marinade. Stir fry the pork until lightly browned, then add the mushrooms and stir fry for a further 2 – 3 minutes before pouring in the marinade.

Bring the juices to the boil, reduce the heat and pour in the cream. Heat for 1 minute but do not allow the cream to boil. Taste for seasoning.

Arrange the lettuce leaves on a serving platter and spoon the pork mixture into them. Garnish with tarragon, if liked, and serve at once.

Turkey Nests

You need to have two fine metal sieves or a special frying basket to make the nests in which to serve this stir fry. If you do not want to go to all the trouble of making the nests, the stir fry may also be served in crispy baked potato shells, pastry shells – as in Turkey and Broccoli Tartlets – or pancakes.

SERVES 4

175–225 g/6–8 oz Chinese egg noodles (see Cook's Tip)
oil for deep frying
100 g/4 oz cream cheese
2 tbsp chopped fresh parsley
1 tsp chopped fresh thyme
1 tsp grated lemon rind
2 tbsp olive oil
450 g/1 lb boneless turkey breast, finely shredded

1 red pepper, seeded and finely shredded
salt and freshly ground black pepper
100 g/4 oz fine green beans, blanced in boiling water for 1 minute
100 g/4 oz lean cooked ham, shredded

Add the noodles to boiling water and bring back to the boil. Drain and rinse under cold water. Drain well.

Thoroughly grease two metal sieves: one measuring about 2.5 cm/1 in larger than the other. The larger sieve should be about 10 cm/4 in in diameter – no bigger. Heat the oil for deep frying. Line the larger sieve with a layer of noodles and press the smaller one inside to hold the noodles in place. Deep fry the noodles until golden, then remove them from the sieves and leave to drain on absorbent kitchen paper. Make eight nests. The nests can be made in advance and reheated in a very hot oven for a few minutes before serving – they must be crisp

Mix the cream cheese, parsley, thyme and lemon rind, then shape into eight small pats and chill them.

Heat the oil, then stir fry the turkey and pepper, adding seasoning, until the turkey is lightly browned and the pepper tender. Stir in the beans and continue cooking for 3 minutes to heat them through. Lastly, add the ham and cook for a minute or so.

Divide the stir fried mixture between the nests and top each with a pat of flavoured cream cheese. Serve at once.

COOK'S TIP

About 100 g/4 oz noodles will make 5 nests; therefore 225 g/8 oz will make 10 nests; this allows for breakages.

Turkey and Broccoli Tartlets

The tartlets may be made well ahead and heated through gently just before serving.

SERVES 4

225 g/8 oz plain flour
175 g/6 oz butter
4 tbsp cranberry sauce
2 tbsp sunflower oil
225 g/8 oz boneless turkey breast, cut into fine strips

salt and freshly ground black pepper
100 g/4 oz broccoli florets, broken into small pieces
50 g/2 oz walnuts, chopped
2 spring onions, chopped
4 tbsp double cream
a little chopped fresh parsley

Set the oven at 200°C, 400°F, gas 6. Place the flour in a bowl and rub in the butter, then mix in just enough water to bind the ingredients into a dough. Roll out and use it to line four individual, loose-bottomed flan tins. Prick the base of the pastry all over, then chill the cases for 30 minutes.

Place a piece of greaseproof paper and some dried peas or baking beans in each tartlet, and bake for 20 minutes. Remove the beans and paper and cook for a further 5 – 10 minutes, or until the pastry is golden.

Spread a little cranberry sauce in each tartlet. Heat the oil and stir fry the turkey, adding seasoning, until lightly browned. Stir in the broccoli, walnuts and spring onions and continue stir frying for a further 3 – 5 minutes, until the broccoli is bright and slightly tender.

Fill the tartlets with the turkey mixture and spoon a little cream over each one. Sprinkle with parsley.

Veal with Vermouth

A bowl of buttered noodles and a salad will taste good with this simple veal dish.

SERVES 4

4 veal escalopes, beaten out thinly, then cut into strips
3 tbsp plain flour
salt and freshly ground black pepper
2 tbsp oil
knob of butter
100 g/4 oz rindless smoked bacon rashers, diced
1 small onion, thinly sliced

250 ml/8 fl oz dry white vermouth
425 g/15 oz can artichoke hearts, drained
4 tbsp double cream
100 g/4 oz black grapes, halved and deseeded (if necessary)

GARNISH (OPTIONAL)
4 small sprigs of grapes
fresh herbs

Toss the veal with the flour and seasoning. Heat the oil and butter, then stir fry the bacon and onion for 5 minutes. Add the veal and continue to stir fry until the strips of meat are lightly browned.

Pour in the vermouth and bring to the boil, stirring all the time. Add the artichoke hearts and simmer for 3 minutes. Stir in the cream and grapes, then transfer the cooked veal to a serving dish or individual plates. Garnish with grapes and fresh herbs, if liked.

AS AN ASIDE

Stir fried accompaniments can pep up long-cooked main dishes adding contrasting colour, texture and a fresh, zingy flavour. Consider these recipes too, when you plan a barbecue or buffet-style lunch, stirring them up at the last minute to refresh plain or cold centrepieces.

The dishes include satisfying rice, grains and bean ensembles, as well as light vegetable mixtures. If you are looking for an interesting, simple supper dish, you may even find the right candidate here by serving simple vegetable combinations as a topping for fresh cooked pasta.

Use the information in the recipes to create very simple side dishes, combining one or two vegetables with some herbs or seasoning. Let the flavour of the fresh ingredients dominate the dish and you will not be far away from perfect results.

Summer Vegetables

This refreshing mixture of yellow vegetables is interesting enough to transform plain, cooked pasta into a complete meal. It also turns plain, grilled fish, poultry or meat into a splendid main course.

SERVES 4

225 g/8 oz baby corn cobs
3 tbsp olive oil
1 yellow pepper, seeded and thinly sliced
1 small onion, halved and thinly sliced
4 yellow courgettes, thinly sliced

6 yellow tomatoes, halved, seeded and cut in thin strips
salt and freshly ground black pepper
handful of basil leaves
1 tbsp grated lemon rind
3 tbsp chopped fresh parsley
1 small garlic clove, finely chopped (optional)

Cover the corn cobs with water and bring them to the boil. Continue to boil for 2 minutes, then drain the corn and set aside.

Heat the oil, then stir fry the pepper and onion for 5 – 8 minutes, until softened. Add the corn and continue to stir fry for another 5 minutes or until the corn and onion are cooked, but still slightly crunchy.

Toss in the courgettes and tomatoes and stir fry for about 3 minutes – just long enough to heat the vegetables and take the raw edge off the courgettes. Sprinkle in seasoning to taste and the basil leaves, and mix well. Turn the vegetables into a serving dish or individual side plates. Mix the lemon rind, parsley and garlic, if liked, then sprinkle this mixture over the vegetables. Serve at once.

Winter Stir Fry

This tasty root vegetable mixture goes well with simple foods like poached or fried eggs, grilled bacon or other grilled meats.

SERVES 4

2 large potatoes, coarsely grated
2 large carrots, coarsely grated
1 parsnip, coarsely grated
2 tbsp plain flour
salt and pepper

4 tbsp oil
1 large onion, chopped
225 g/8 oz white cabbage, finely shredded

Rinse the potatoes under plenty of cold water, then drain them and squeeze out excess moisture so that the shreds separate. Mix the potatoes with the carrots and parsnip. Sprinkle in the flour and plenty of seasoning, then toss the vegetable shreds with the flour using a fork.

Heat the oil and stir fry the onion for 3 minutes. Add the grated vegetables and stir fry for about 15 minutes, or until they are lightly browned. As the vegetables are cooking they should be turned over and mixed from the centre outwards, and from the sides of the pan to the middle, so that the shreds brown and stay separate. If the vegetables are stirred in a circular direction they will brown underneath, and they tend to stick together in a large clump.

Add the cabbage and continue to stir fry for another 5 – 7 minutes, or until the cabbage is lightly cooked and the other vegetables are browned. Serve at once.

WINTER STIR FRY

Rice with Spinach

SERVES 4

175 g/6 oz long-grain rice,
  cooked
3 tbsp oil
½ small onion, chopped

2 tbsp cumin seeds
1 tsp turmeric
knob of butter (optional)
225 g/8 oz fresh spinach, cooked,
  drained and shredded

The rice should be freshly cooked and drained if necessary. If cooked by the absorption method, do not fork up the grains but leave the pan covered off the heat when the rice is cooked.

Heat the oil and stir fry the onion with the cumin seeds for 5 minutes. Stir in the turmeric and continue to cook for 2 minutes before adding the butter, if used. Allow the butter to melt, then add the rice and stir fry for 2 minutes until it has become well coated in the flavouring ingredients.

Make a well in the rice or push it to one side of the pan and add the spinach. Stir fry the spinach briefly to heat it through. Then fork the spinach into the rice and serve at once.

Cucumber with Ham

Another quick stir fry to serve as a side dish or with some rice or pasta, or in a baked potato as a light main course. This is delicious with poached or grilled chicken or turkey.

SERVES 4

1 cucumber, peeled, halved
  lengthways and sliced (about
  450 g/1 lb)
salt and freshly ground black
  pepper

225 g/8 oz lean cooked ham, cut
  into small cubes
3 spring onions, chopped
2 tsp paprika
2 tbsp oil
1 garlic clove, crushed (optional)

The cucumber slices should be about 3 mm/⅛ in thick. Place them in a colander or sieve and sprinkle with a little salt, then leave over a bowl to drain for 15 minutes. Pat all the slices dry on absorbent kitchen paper.

Place the ham in a bowl with the spring onions. Add the paprika and a little freshly ground black pepper, then mix well to coat the ham in the seasoning.

Heat the oil, then stir fry the garlic, if used, and ham for 5 minutes to lightly brown the meat and seal on the seasoning. Add the cucumber and continue stir frying for another 5 minutes, to lightly cook the vegetable. Serve at once.

RICE WITH SPINACH

SLIGHTLY SPICY LEEKS

Slightly Spicy Leeks

I like the combination of orange, leek and spice –
particularly with grilled or barbecued mackerel, duck,
sausages, gammon or pork. However, if the orange
clashes with your main dish it may be omitted or the
rind of half a lemon may be added instead.

SERVES 4

4 tbsp oil
2 tbsp crushed coriander seeds
grated rind and juice of 1 orange
¼ tsp ground allspice

450 g/1 lb leeks, thinly sliced and
    separated into rings
salt and freshly ground black
    pepper

Heat the oil, then stir fry the crushed coriander with the
orange rind and allspice over fairly low heat for 2 – 3
minutes, or until the orange rind is quite bright and the
mixture is fragrant.

Toss in all the leeks and increase the heat, then stir
fry the vegetables for about 8 minutes, or until they are
softened. Add the orange juice and boil hard for 2
minutes, tossing the leeks to coat them in a spicy glaze.
Taste and add seasoning, then serve at once.

Celeriac with Peas

Celeriac is a swede-like vegetable with thick, pale skin
and a crunchy texture. It has a mild celery flavour and is
excellent eaten raw or cooked, making it an ideal stir fry
candidate.

SERVES 6

1 small to medium celeriac root,
    peeled and cut in short thin
    strips
juice of ½ lemon
2 tbsp olive oil

1 small leek, cut in short strips
225 g/8 oz shelled peas, frozen or
    blanched fresh
a little freshly grated nutmeg
salt and freshly ground black
    pepper

Cut the celeriac into pieces, placing it in a bowl of cold
water with the lemon juice added to prevent it
discolouring.

Heat the oil and stir fry the leek for about 3 minutes.
Drain the celeriac, shake off the water and add it to the
leek. Stir fry fairly vigorously for 5 minutes, then add the
peas and continue to stir fry for another 5 minutes. The
peas should be just cooked and the celeriac should still
be crisp. Add a little nutmeg and seasoning to taste
before serving the vegetables.

RICE AND BEANS

🥘 Rice and Beans

SERVES 4 – 6

2 tbsp oil
1 large onion, chopped
2 celery sticks, thinly sliced
1 garlic clove, crushed
2 tbsp sunflower seeds
2 tbsp sesame seeds
2 × 425 g/15 oz cans red kidney
  beans, drained

2 tsp dried marjoram
salt and freshly ground black
  pepper
175 g/6 oz long-grain brown or
  white rice, freshly cooked
4 tbsp chopped parsley

Heat the oil, then stir fry the onion, celery and garlic for 10 – 15 minutes until the onion is softened, but not browned. Stir in the seeds and continue to cook for 2 minutes. Add the beans, marjoram and seasoning, and stir fry for a further 2 – 3 minutes to heat them through.

Tip in the rice and stir fry it for a few minutes to combine the ingredients and allow the flavours to mingle. Fork in the parsley and serve at once.

COOK'S TIP

This is a good way of using up leftover cooked rice. However, remember that the rice should be thoroughly heated before serving, therefore it should be stir fried for longer.

🥘 Piquant Green Beans

If using frozen beans for this stir fry, there is no need to blanch them before frying. If fresh dill is not available, don't bother with dried dill weed – it is better to use fresh parsley instead.

SERVES 4

450 g/1 lb fine French beans,
  trimmed
1 tbsp olive oil
1 tbsp sunflower oil
½ small onion, finely chopped

1 pickled cucumber, diced
1 tbsp capers, chopped
salt and freshly ground black
  pepper
2 eggs, hard-boiled and chopped
2 tbsp chopped fresh dill

Plunge the beans into boiling water, bring the water back to the boil, then drain the beans. Heat both oils, then stir fry the onion and cucumber for about 3 minutes, until the onion is slightly softened.

Stir in the beans, capers and seasoning. Continue to stir fry for a further 3 minutes or until the beans are hot and cooked, but still crunchy. Transfer to a serving dish or individual plates and sprinkle with the egg and dill. Serve at once.

Spinach with Apples and Walnuts

SERVES 4

450 g/1 lb fresh spinach
3 tbsp olive oil
½ small onion, finely chopped
2 full-flavoured eating apples,
    peeled, cored and diced
75 g/3 oz walnut pieces, chopped
knob of butter (optional)
salt and freshly ground black
    pepper

Wash the spinach, then place it dripping wet in a large pan. Cover with a lid and cook over high heat, shaking the pan often, for about 3 minutes, or until the spinach has reduced in volume and softened. Drain well, pressing all the liquid from the spinach.

Heat the oil, then stir fry the onion and apples until the onion has softened, but not browned. Stir in the nuts and continue stir frying for about 5 minutes to roast them and bring out their flavour. Add the butter and heat it through before adding the spinach. Stir fry the spinach for 3 minutes. Add seasoning to taste and then serve at once.

Carrots with Caraway

This may be made using old carrots, in which case they should be cut into small sticks (they do not have to be as fine as julienne) or into even slices. If caraway is not your favourite spice, try substituting fennel seeds instead – they are also good with carrots and orange.

SERVES 4 – 6

450 g/1 lb whole baby carrots
2 tbsp olive oil
1 small onion, finely chopped
1 tbsp caraway seeds
knob of butter (optional)
juice of 1 large orange

Plunge the carrots into just enough boiling water to cover them and bring the water back to the boil. Boil for 2 minutes, then drain the carrots.

Heat the oil and stir fry the onion with the caraway seeds until the onion is softened, but not browned. Add the butter, if used, and allow it to melt. Tip the carrots into the pan and stir fry them for 3 minutes before adding the orange juice.

Boil the orange juice rapidly, turning the carrots all the time, until it is reduced to a slightly caramelized glaze which coats the vegetables. The carrots should be crunchy but not hard, and they should be coated in a full-flavoured glaze. Serve at once.

SPINACH WITH APPLES AND WALNUTS

Chop Suey

Use this as a basis for a variety of dishes – stir fry shredded raw chicken breast, pork or beef before adding the vegetables to make a main course dish. Alternatively, add some peeled cooked prawns (thawed if frozen) with the beansprouts. Also, the combination of vegetables may be changed to suit the season or the contents of the salad drawer in the refrigerator – remember, however, that beansprouts are the essential ingredient for a chop suey.

SERVES 4

2 tsp cornflour	1 celery stick, cut into fine short strips
2 tbsp soy sauce	1 green pepper, seeded and cut into fine short strips
1 tbsp dry sherry	
2 tbsp oil	½ onion, thinly sliced
1 tsp sesame oil	350 g/12 oz beansprouts

Blend the cornflour with the soy sauce, sherry and 2 tablespoons of water; set aside.

Heat both oils together, then stir fry the celery, pepper and onion for 5 minutes. The vegetables should be lightly cooked and still crunchy. Toss in the beansprouts and stir fry for 1 minute. Give the cornflour mixture a stir, pour it into the pan and bring the juices to the boil, stirring all the time. Cook for 2 minutes, stirring, then serve at once.

CHOP SUEY

PUMPKIN WITH LEEKS

Pumpkin with Leeks

I find that stir frying is one of the best cooking methods for pumpkin – the vegetable remains whole but slightly tender. Turn this into a tasty supper dish by stir frying some diced, rindless bacon with the leeks.

SERVES 4

2 tbsp oil	50 g/2 oz sultanas
knob of butter	450 g/1 lb prepared pumpkin flesh, cubed
1 garlic clove, crushed (optional)	salt and freshly ground black pepper
2 leeks, sliced	
2 tsp ground cinnamon	

Heat the oil and butter until the butter melts, then add the garlic (if wished), leeks, cinnamon and sultanas. Stir fry the leeks for 5 minutes until they are softened.

Add the pumpkin and seasoning. Continue stir frying until the cubes are tender, but not soft enough to become mushy, which takes about 7 – 10 minutes. Serve the dish at once.

Beetroot with Horseradish

SERVES 4

4 tbsp oil
2 onions, halved and thinly sliced
450 g/1 lb cooked beetroot, cut
  in small cubes

salt and freshly ground black
  pepper
3 tbsp chopped fresh dill
4 tbsp horseradish sauce
100 ml/4 fl oz soured cream

Heat the oil and stir fry the onions for 10 minutes, until they are quite well cooked and beginning to brown. Add the beetroot with seasoning and continue to stir fry for about 5 minutes for the beetroot to become hot, and for the flavour of the onions to mingle with it. Stir in the dill and transfer the beetroot to a serving dish.

Mix the horseradish sauce with the soured cream and trickle this over the beetroot. Serve at once, tossing the horseradish cream with the beetroot and onion as the vegetables are spooned out.

CORIANDER POTATOES

Coriander Potatoes

Coriander is one of my favourite spices – it works wonders for new potatoes, complementing their sweet fresh flavour perfectly.

SERVES 4

900 g/2 lb small new potatoes, scrubbed and boiled
salt and freshly ground black pepper
2 tsp caster sugar

2 tbsp lemon juice
4 tbsp olive oil
3 tbsp crushed coriander seeds
strip of lemon
4 tbsp snipped chives

Cook the potatoes in boiling, slightly salted water for 10 – 15 minutes, or until tender. Drain. Stir the sugar and lemon juice together until the sugar dissolves.

Heat the oil and stir fry the coriander for 2 minutes. Add the lemon rind and continue to cook for a further minute, pressing the piece of rind to bring out its flavour. Tip the potatoes into the pan and then stir fry them for about 10 minutes, or until they are just beginning to brown on the outside.

Pour the sweetened lemon juice over the potatoes and mix them well with the oil in the pan, so that the liquids mingle to form a hot dressing. Mix in the chives, check the seasoning and serve at once.

Cracked Wheat with Courgettes

Do not confuse cracked wheat with bulgur – cracked wheat is broken not cooked.

SERVES 4

100 g/4 oz cracked wheat
4 tbsp olive oil
strip of lemon rind
1 bay leaf
2 rosemary sprigs
1 onion, finely chopped

25 g/1 oz slivered almonds
225 g/8 oz small courgettes, thinly sliced
salt and black pepper
plenty of chopped fresh parsley
lemon wedges to serve (optional)

Heat the oil, then stir fry the lemon rind, bay leaf, rosemary and onion for about 10 minutes, or until the onion is softened and the herbs release their flavour. Add the slivered almonds after 5 minutes so that they are lightly browned at the end of this stage.

Next add the courgettes and stir fry them for about 2 minutes, so that they are very lightly cooked – this way their flavour will be at its best. Sprinkle in seasoning, then tip the cracked wheat into the pan. Stir well for a minute or so to mix the ingredients.

Add plenty of chopped parsley and remove the herb sprigs if you prefer before serving, or pick out the herbs to garnish the top of the wheat mixture. Lemon wedges may be served so that their juice can be squeezed over the courgettes and wheat just before eating.
Put the wheat in a sieve and rinse it well under cold, running water. Place the grain in a pan with plenty of cold water. Bring to the boil and reduce the heat so that the water simmers. Cook the wheat for 20 minutes until tender. Drain and set aside.

Cauliflower and Celery Stir Fry

SERVES 4 – 6

3 tbsp oil
1 small onion, halved and thinly sliced
½ small cauliflower, broken into small florets
1 celery heart, thinly sliced
salt and freshly ground black pepper
50 g/2 oz stoned black olives, sliced
1 sweet eating apple, cored and roughly chopped
1 tbsp capers, chopped
1 tbsp demerara sugar
1 – 2 tbsp cider vinegar

Heat the oil and stir fry the onion for 5 minutes before adding the cauliflower and celery. Stir fry the vegetables until they are lightly cooked – they should not taste raw but should still be crunchy. This takes about 15 minutes, depending on the heat and the size of the pan.

Add seasoning, the olives, apple, capers, and continue to stir fry for 2 minutes. Make a well in the middle of the vegetables and add the sugar and 1 tablespoon of the vinegar. Stir the juices until the sugar dissolves, then toss the small amount of dressing with the vegetables. Taste and add the remaining vinegar if liked. Serve at once.

Broccoli with Avocado

SERVES 4

450 g/1 lb young broccoli spears, cut in small pieces
2 avocados, halved, stoned, peeled and diced
juice of ½ lemon
3 tbsp olive oil
2 spring onions, chopped
salt and freshly ground black pepper
a few basil sprigs, leaves removed

Trim any long stalks from the broccoli and chop these to ensure that all the vegetable is evenly cooked. Toss the avocados in the lemon juice to prevent discoloration.

Heat the oil, then stir fry the broccoli and spring onions for about 5 minutes, or until cooked but still firm. Add seasoning and the avocados, then stir fry for another minute or so to heat the avocado. Toss in the basil leaves and serve at once.

CAULIFLOWER AND CELERY STIR FRY

STIRRING SWEETS

The idea of stir frying a dessert may seem a little bizarre and I have to admit that it is a bit of a gimmick; however, these stir fries are all recipes that would excite gastric juices rather than raise eyebrows if they went by a cooking method of any other name.

Based mainly on fruit, the combinations of flavourings and serving ideas certainly do not stretch stir frying beyond sensible limits. Since fruit reacts with uncoated metal, a carbon steel wok is not the ideal cooking pan for many of these recipes – better to use a large frying pan or skillet. Do not shy away from making this the second stir fry of the meal – as long as your choice of ingredients is balanced, the method is unlikely to dominate and cause a clash. Do remember to have a clean pan ready though. Since many fruits discolour if they are cut and exposed to air for any length of time, sprinkle prepared ingredients with a little lemon juice and cover closely if you are preparing them in advance.

PEARS WITH CASSIS

Pears with Cassis

SERVES 4

8 small, firm pears, peeled, cored
   and quartered
juice of 1 large orange
knob of unsalted butter
100 ml/4 fl oz cassis (blackcurrant
   liqueur)

4 tbsp flaked almonds, toasted
sprigs of blackcurrants or halved
   orange slices to decorate
whipped cream to serve

Toss the pears in the orange juice. Melt the butter, then add the pears, reserving the juice, and stir fry until they are softened but still retaining their shape.

Pour the orange juice and cassis over the pears and mix well to coat all the pieces of fruit in sauce. Transfer to four dishes and sprinkle each portion with flaked almonds. Decorate with blackcurrant sprigs or halved orange slices when blackcurrants are not available. Serve at once, with whipped cream.

Maple Fruits

The pears should be quite firm, but not hard and crunchy in texture.

SERVES 4

4 firm pears, peeled, cored and
   thickly sliced lengthways
2 firm, ripe peaches, peeled,
   stoned and thickly sliced

juice of 1 lemon
50 g/2 oz unsalted butter
225 g/8 oz strawberries
6 tbsp maple syrup

Toss the pears and peaches in lemon juice as they are prepared, keeping them separate. Melt the butter and stir fry the pears over a fairly high heat until they are lightly browned around the edges.

Add the peach slices and continue stir frying for a minute or so to heat them through. Stir in the strawberries, any remaining lemon juice and the maple syrup. Stir the fruit briefly to coat all the pieces in syrup. Divide the fruits between four dishes and serve at once.

COOK'S TIP

To peel peaches, place them in a heatproof bowl and pour freshly boiling water over to cover the fruit. Leave to stand for about 1 minute: firm fruit may need 1½ – 2 minutes to loosen the skin whereas ripe fruit may be ready after 45 seconds. If the fruit is allowed to stand too long it will begin to cook and become soft.

Drain the peaches and slit the skin with the point of a knife, then it should peel off easily. Remember to toss cut or peeled peaches in lemon juice to prevent them from discolouring.

Strange Carrot Dessert

The idea for this unusual recipe stems from the Indian dessert of carrot halva.

SERVES 4 – 6

50 g/2 oz unsalted butter
50 g/2 oz slivered almonds
450 g/1 lb carrots, finely grated
100 g/4 oz caster sugar
2 tbsp rose water
juice of 3 oranges
whipped cream to serve

Melt the butter and stir fry the almonds until they are lightly browned. Use a slotted spoon to remove them from the pan, drain them on absorbent kitchen paper and set aside.

Add the carrots to the butter remaining in the pan and stir fry them for 15 minutes, or until they are a deep golden colour. Stir in the sugar and rose water, and stir fry until the sugar melts. Continue cooking, adding a little orange juice every few minutes to keep the carrots moist. When all the orange juice is added, carry on stir frying the mixture until the excess moisture has evaporated and the carrot shreds are soft and juicy – 10 – 15 minutes in total.

Transfer the carrot mixture to a serving dish and top with the almonds. Allow to cool until just warm, then serve topped with whipped cream. Alternatively, the carrot mixture may be chilled and served cold.

STRANGE CARROT DESSERT

COEUR A LA CREME WITH SPICED PLUMS

Coeur à la Crème with Spiced Plums

Traditionally, *coeur à la crème* is set in small heart-shaped moulds with perforated bases. The drained cheese mixture is firm enough to turn out. Prepare the *coeur à la crème* a day ahead so that it has sufficient time to drain and set.

SERVES 4

225 g/8 oz curd cheese
4 tbsp caster sugar
150 ml/¼ pint whipping cream, lightly whipped
knob of butter
450 g/1 lb firm plums, halved and stoned
2 tsp ground cinnamon
¼ tsp ground cloves
½ tsp ground mixed spice
100 g/4 oz sugar

Beat the curd cheese and sugar together, then fold in the whipped cream. Line the base of four ramekin dishes with a circle of greaseproof paper. Divide the cheese mixture between the dishes, pressing it down flat. Cover with muslin, tying it in place securely (or use elastic bands). Invert the dishes on a wire rack and stand the rack in a dish. Chill the cheeses for 24 hours.

To serve the cheeses, remove the muslin and slide the blade of a knife around the inside of the dishes to loosen the cheeses. Invert each one in turn onto an individual serving plate. Chill until the plums are cooked.

Melt the butter and stir fry the plums for 1 minute. Add all the spices and continue stir frying for a further 2 minutes. Tip in the sugar and cook, stirring less briskly, until the juice runs from the plums and the sugar dissolves to form a spicy syrup.

Arrange the spiced plums on the plates alongside the *coeur à la crème* and serve immediately.

Yogurt Delight

SERVES 4

750 ml/1¼ pints Greek yogurt
grated rind and juice of 1 orange
3 – 4 tbsp clear honey
knob of unsalted butter
50 g/2 oz shelled pistachio nuts
50 g/2 oz Brazil nuts, roughly
    chopped

4 tbsp raisins
2 firm pears, peeled, cored and
    diced
100 g/4 oz ready-to-eat dried
    apricots, sliced
50 g/2 oz seedless grapes, halved

Mix the yogurt, orange rind and 1 – 2 tablespoons of the honey, then divide it between four dishes and chill well.

Melt the butter, then stir fry the pistachios and Brazils with the raisins for 3 minutes. Add the pears and continue to stir fry for about 3 minutes, or until the pears are lightly cooked. Stir in the apricots and orange juice and bring to the boil. Boil, stirring, for 2 minutes to reduce the orange juice.

Stir in the grapes and remaining honey (or to taste) and heat through briefly. Spoon the fruit and nut mixture on top of the chilled yogurt and serve at once.

Ratafia Cherries

Ratafia biscuits are miniature almond macaroons, usually on sale in delicatessen shops or larger supermarkets.

SERVES 4

50 g/2 oz unsalted butter
450 g/1 lb cherries, stoned
1 tbsp clear honey

4 tbsp kirsch
100 g/4 oz ratafia biscuits
whipped cream, fromage frais or
    natural yogurt to serve

Melt the butter and stir fry the cherries for 3–5 minutes until they begin to change colour, but do not burst and become too soft.

Stir in the honey and kirsch and toss the fruit well to coat it in the sauce. Remove the pan from the heat, add the ratafia biscuits and mix them in briskly. Immediately spoon the fruit and biscuit mixture into four serving dishes. Top each portion with cream, fromage frais or yogurt, then serve at once.

YOGURT DELIGHT

Banana and Avocado Crunch

SERVES 4

2 ripe avocados
2 bananas
juice of 1 lemon
2 tbsp icing sugar
150 ml/¼ pint whipping cream, whipped

50 g/2 oz unsalted butter
4 thick slices white bread, crusts removed and made into breadcrumbs
75 g/3 oz walnut pieces, chopped
4 tbsp demerara sugar
1 tsp ground cinnamon

Halve, stone and peel the avocado. Mash the avocado flesh with the bananas and lemon juice. Stir in the icing sugar. Reserve some of the whipped cream for decorating, spooning it into a piping bag fitted with a star nozzle. Fold the rest of the cream into the avocado mixture. Cover and chill.

Melt the butter and stir fry the breadcrumbs until they are golden brown and crisp. Stir in the walnuts, sugar and cinnamon, and continue to cook briefly. Allow to cool slightly.

Place a layer of avocado mixture in four dishes, then divide half the crumb mixture between them. Top with the remaining avocado mixture, then cover with the rest of the crumbs. Decorate with swirls of whipped cream and serve at once.

BANANA AND AVOCADO CRUNCH

MANGO AND BANANA SLICES

Mango and Banana Slices

SERVES 4

4 slices plain cake
4 tbsp sherry
50 g/2 oz unsalted butter
1 ripe, but firm, mango peeled, stoned and sliced

3 tbsp redcurrant jelly
3 bananas, sliced
2 tbsp orange juice

Divide the cake slices between four plates and sprinkle a spoonful of sherry over each portion.

Melt half the butter and stir fry the mango slices for 1 – 2 minutes, until they are hot. Add the redcurrant jelly and continue stir frying for a minute or so until the jelly melts and coats the mango. Divide the mango slices between the four plates, arranging them on top of the cake. Scrape all the juices from the pan over the mango.

Melt the remaining butter and briskly stir fry the banana slices until hot. Sprinkle the orange juice over the banana, then stir for a few seconds to heat the juices. Spoon the bananas over the mango slices and serve at once.

Custards with Caramelized Fruit

Vary the fruit according to the season or your budget – combine exotics, such as mango, pawpaw and mangosteen with chunks of pear or pineapple; or cook some apples until golden and add some raisins and a swirl of rum.

SERVES 4

600 ml/1 pint of milk
2 eggs
2 egg yolks
3 tbsp sugar
knob of unsalted butter
1 tbsp walnut oil

1 pineapple, peeled, cored and cubed
4 tbsp orange juice
75 g/3 oz dark soft brown sugar
4 oranges, peeled and segments removed

Set the oven at 170°C, 325°F, gas 3. Have a roasting tin ready to hold the dishes of custard and a kettle of boiling water. Butter four ramekin dishes. Heat the milk until almost boiling, then remove from the heat.

Beat the eggs and yolks with the sugar, then whisk in the milk. Strain the custards into the four dishes and stand them in the roasting tin. Pour in boiling water to two-thirds of the way up the sides of the ramekin dishes. Cover with greased greaseproof paper and bake for 40 minutes, or until the custards are set. Leave to cool in the tin, then chill well, preferably overnight.

Invert the custards on to four serving plates before stir frying the pineapple. Melt the butter with the walnut oil, then stir fry the pineapple for 3 minutes. Add the orange juice and stir in the brown sugar. Continue to cook, stirring, until the sugar melts and the liquid boils. Boil for a few minutes until the syrup is reduced and caramelized.

Remove the pan from the heat and add the orange segments. Spoon the fruit and caramel around and over the custards and serve at once.

Cinnamon Apples and Apricots

SERVES 4

4 eating apples, peeled, cored and quartered
juice of ½ lemon
4 tbsp caster sugar

1 tbsp ground cinnamon
knob of butter
450 g/1 lb fresh apricots, halved and stoned

Toss the apple quarters in lemon juice. Mix the sugar and cinnamon, then toss the moist apple quarters in it to coat them as evenly as possible.

Melt the butter and stir fry the apples until they are lightly caramelized outside. Add the apricots and continue stir frying for about 3 minutes, depending on the ripeness of the apricots, until the apricot halves are tender and hot. Transfer to four serving dishes and serve at once.

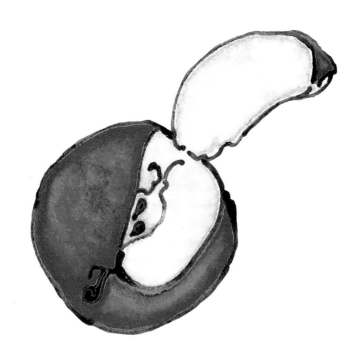

INDEX